Listen to what other women Lofaro and *Slices of Life:*

"Ellie Lofaro is a vivacious and gifted Christian communicator. *Slices of Life* contains warm humor, interesting stories, keen insights for our lives in Christ, and more than a few good chuckles—a moving and engaging read."
—**Mrs. Charles Colson**

"Humor. Wisdom. Wit. Ellie Lofaro wraps all three into a glorious package. I've admired her speaking gifts for years, and now it's clear she possesses the eloquence and talent of a seasoned author. This book is about real life and a real Savior. What a gift!"
—**Kathy Troccoli**, Recording artist, author, and speaker

"Even a reserved Anglo-Saxon could not stop the belly laughs from constantly welling up while reading Slices of Life. My endorphins are replenished; my heart is warmed. Ellic Lofaro has given us a gift."
—**Dee Brestin**, Speaker and author

"I LOVE THIS BOOK! It's a combination of inspiration and encouragement with peaks of laughter. Ellie's writing has a FRESH flavor—no old ideas churned up, but exciting fresh quality with deep insights about marriage, kids, life, and God. Her convictions are thought-provoking and yet have a lighthearted touch, which helps the truth sink in."
—**Barbara Johnson**, Best-selling author, Women of Faith speaker, founder of Spatula Ministries

"After reading *Slices of Life*, I wanted to chat with Ellie over a cappuccino and some tiramisu! Her stories made me laugh, but most importantly, the reminded me of the common bond we women share and my need to live out my faith in every 'slice of life' God sends my way."
—**Jane Johnson Struck**, Editor, *Today's Christian Woman* magazine

"Ellie's *Slices of Life* reads like a giant kaleidoscope: her vibrant writing, her colorful confessions, and her Scriptural insights sparkle! Out of the everydayness and the brokenness of life come lovely patterns of light as Ellie spins her gift of storytelling—and we girlfriends get to view the brilliant results.
—**Patsy Clairmont**, Best-selling author and Women of Faith speaker

Slices of Life

Unexpected Blessings from Everyday Life

Ellie Lofaro

4/1/11

Francie—

Be blessed!

xo
Ellie

David C Cook®

transforming lives together

SLICES OF LIFE
Published by David C. Cook
4050 Lee Vance View
Colorado Springs, CO 80918 U.S.A.

David C. Cook Distribution Canada
55 Woodslee Avenue, Paris, Ontario, Canada N3L 3E5

David C. Cook U.K., Kingsway Communications
Eastbourne, East Sussex BN23 6NT, England

David C. Cook and the graphic circle C logo
are registered trademarks of Cook Communications Ministries.

Library of Congress Cataloging-in-Publication Data
Lofaro, Ellie.
Slices of life : unexpected blessings from real relationships /
Ellie Lofaro.
p. cm.
Includes bibliographical references.
ISBN 0-7814-3743-1
1. Christian women--Religious life--Humor. 2. Lofaro,
Ellie--Humor. I. Title.
BV4527 .L64 2002
248.8'43'0207--dc21   2001005312

©2002 Ellie Lofaro
Editor: Janet Lee
Design: Alan Furst
Background Cover photo: Alan Furst
Inset Cover photo: © Tom & Dee Ann McCarthy/The Stock Market

Printed in the United States of America
First Edition 2003

2 3 4 5 6 7 8 9 10

033108

Table of Contents

Acknowledgments

My heartfelt thanks to . . .

Frank Lofaro, a "real man." Honey, I'd marry you all over again. Thank you for being a safe place, a rock, and an occasional muzzle. I love you.

My wonderful children, **Paris, Jordan,** and **Capri.** You are the source of so much joy. Through you, I have learned the meaning of unconditional love.

My Buddy; **Kathy Troccoli.** We've seen the best, the worst, the deepest parts of both our hearts . . . every day I treasure you more.

My Prayer Partners. I would never be able to do what I do without your intercession. Your prayers are the most perfect gift of love. I am humbled.

The Church Ladies in New York. Your nurturing spirits have helped me find my destiny. I miss you. I wish you could all move to Virginia. Visit soon and bring pizza.

The Church Ladies in Virginia. Thanks for welcoming in a stranger. It's so good to belong.

The Bright Pond Bible Study, for having humble hearts, open minds, and willing spirits. You cause much rejoicing in heaven—and in me.

D Group, for three years of truth, transparency, and tears. You are all very brave. Remember to put your armor on. D Group is "D" best!

Ramona Tucker, Jane Johnson Struck, and **Anne Spangler,** for giving a chance to a new kid. You have opened many doors. I am grateful.

Lloyd Parker, for making a talk show host out of me, and **Brad Crook,** for making a columnist out of me. What fun it's been.

Jim Galvin of Galvin Associates. You cleared the land and smoothed the path leading up to it. Your counsel is deeply appreciated.

My gifted editor, **Janet Lee.** Thanks for offering a good eye, an open ear, and a very kind heart. Our conversations always bless me.

Cook Communications Ministries, for having the vision and the vehicle to encourage people with the Great News.

A humble offering of worship and praise goes to my Savior, Jesus.

Thank you for my life, Lord. I know why I'm here.

This book is dedicated to
Alessandra D'Alberti Bermani Mannarino
Una buona donna,
una buona Cristiana,
e una buona amica.

I love you, Mom.

Preface

I occupy a very small corner of the world. I've been walking around in it for over forty years, but I'm just beginning to truly enter the promised land. It's been a unique journey in some ways and a common one in others. You and I are one on so many levels—fellow sojourners on an ever-changing road. We discover hills and valleys, pitfalls and plateaus, lush meadows and brush fires. The joys and sorrows are continually interspersed. The challenges never seem to end.

I have learned the greatest revelations along this road often come through observing the mundane. Whether in the ordinary or the extraordinary, the Spirit of God can be intimately met. His face can be seen. His voice can be heard. His touch can be felt. He is in the conversation with a six-year-old as well as in the great sermon. He comes along in the car pool as well as on the missions trip. He promises that if we seek Him, He can be found.

Only when we give up fashioning Him in our own image will we discover that He is everywhere—in every situation—at every turn in our journey. At times, we presume to know His ways and we draw conclusions, make predictions, and cast judgments. Spiritual smugness is a dangerous thing—I have learned that the hard way. Our human natures are often opposed to that which is divine. We are so rarely aware of His presence.

But God is full of surprises! He continues to pour out His Spirit where we least expect it. God is precisely where we are so sure He cannot be. He is in our midst. For this I am so grateful—and filled with hope. This hope is reflected in the following forty slices of life. May you sense the Lord's presence in the hard lessons as well as in the lighthearted ones—in laughter as well as tears. You are invited to peek into my predicaments, prayers, and private thoughts. I trust that you will recognize some of them as your own.

1

Bonding with the Blonde Women

llow me to begin at the beginning. I was born in Brooklyn, New York, on October 17, 1957. I was named Elvira Robina Mannarino, and my parents were Albert and Alessandra. We lived on Herkimer Street off Eastern Parkway in the same brownstone where my father grew up with his ten siblings. My family moved to Long Island in the early sixties for a slice of the good life. Thanks to my three brothers, Ronald, Robert, and Richard, I was very athletic and also adept at self-defense. The fifth and final stork delivery produced my sister Michelle—the ally and friend I had always hoped for.

Although New York is often referred to as a huge melting pot, the vast majority (all, to be exact) of my childhood friends were of European ancestry. Like most sprawling suburbs across America at that time, there existed an unspoken wall of segregation. Chances of meeting African-, Asian-, South American-, or Middle Eastern - Americans were slim to none in my white, "Wonder Years" neighborhood. In 1970, we moved to a larger house on a wooded acre, and that home is the setting of my fondest memories from my middle school, high school, and college years.

Most New Yorkers never go too far from the nest. I never imagined that ten years after graduating from Boston College, I would return to the same town I grew up in, but with a husband

and a baby. I embraced marriage and motherhood, and my church became very central to my life. I loved the church and I loved our pastors. I especially loved the women of the church. I admired their strength and their servant hearts. I was often convicted by their "no problem . . . can do" attitudes. These women took Titus 2 seriously, and they freely opened their hearts and homes. I entered both and took plenty of notes.

Read this list of some of my favorite New Yorkers. Read it out loud. Be sure to enunciate every vowel. Stretch out your right hand (palm toward heaven). Cup your fingers. Pronounce each name with feeling and melodic rhythm. Ready? Go ahead.

Josie Greco, Amy Ciofrone, Diane Zarlengo, Marie Gebbia, Judy Conti, Valerie Infranco, Evelyn Zanoni, Michelle Como, Celeste Avolese, Dorothy Rondinelli, Suzanne Azzolini, Debbie Gusmano. Congratulations! You speak fluent Italian! I didn't try to have friends who sound like they're from the cast of a Fellini film. It just turned out that way.

I enjoyed the deep sense of belonging. These dear friends saw me through my early years as a teacher, wife, and mother. They encouraged me in the ever-challenging, sometimes uncomfortable call to take up the cross. It's not that we had a lot of leisure time together. I don't have many memories of "doing lunch." It was the bridal and baby showers, the Bible studies and retreats, and the birthdays and funerals that knit us so tightly together. It was the tears of joy and sorrow shared in the prayer room and at the altar that cemented our lifelong friendships. I knew they would come running if I had a need. What a comfort they had been to me. Then in the summer of 1994, after fifteen years of "belonging," we moved away.

Moving out of state really devastated me. In the past, when I had heard women say things like that, I thought they were wimps. (Open wide, eat, and swallow hard.) It's not that I couldn't function—on the contrary, I threw myself into things full force. I was looking to belong—but there were no takers. I had always proudly proclaimed, "God is all I need." When I left everything and everyone that was familiar, I felt the Lord responding, "Really? Let's see." I later realized the lesson was not to torture me but to test me. The refiner's fire can be very painful, but it produces purity, strength, and value.

Enter "The Blonde Women." I would like to go on record to clarify that my blonde women are not the blonde women from blonde-women jokes. My blonde women are smart, sophisticated, articulate, talented, athletic, accessorized, and very thin. Those are just some of the reasons I didn't like them. Of course they didn't know that. I always made sure I sent mounds of sloppy agape in their direction. I had never encountered the blonde women until we moved to Virginia. The thing that really bugged me the most about the blonde women was that they just smiled and nodded and smiled and nodded. I could never tell what they were thinking. Also, the blonde women never showed any real interest in my children. (Or in me for that matter.) They never hugged or kissed them. Amy Ciofrone used to suck my children's faces, and Celeste Avolese would pinch their cheeks (all four). I miss that. Once in a while, a blonde woman will offer a pat on the head and comment on their dark "I-tally-ann" skin.

I shared some of my blonde women issues a couple of years ago during a ladies luncheon at a wealthy mainline church nearby. The very blonde audience laughed heartily as I shared my frustrations, and they seemed to empathize with my difficulty adjusting. When my message ended and dessert was served (all on fine china), an elegant fifty-something blonde woman made a beeline in my direction. I prepared for the worst. She came uncharacteristically close (for a blonde woman) and declared, "Darling, being blonde is simply a matter of time and money." She winked, grinned knowingly, and walked away.

That's when it hit me. I wasn't able to bond with the blonde women because they were so very different than I was. They looked, acted, spoke, smelled, and walked differently than I did. And their names—even their names were blonde: Linda White, Susan Jones, Lisa Smith, Pam Thompson, Catherine Wilson, Kim Short. (Straight off the roster of the DAR—no relation whatsoever to Fellini.) I had spent almost four decades in settings where there was little or no diversity. I had become accustomed to my own kind (yes, even in a church body), but God had a better way. So you see, it was never about the blonde women—it was always about me. What seemed like aloofness was actually self-control and poise. What seemed like guarded conversation was actually a well-trained tongue. What seemed like formality was a genteel civility. I was thrown into a new culture, and I made the foolish mistake of thinking that the adjustments should be made by everyone else. To top things off, their beauty and poise felt quite threatening. Jokes about health and weight were no longer funny. I began to wonder how I was perceived by the blonde women. (I put one in a headlock until she came clean.) She thought I was arrogant, opinionated, and too inquisitive. I had thought I was confident, clear thinking, and concerned. She said I was aggressive. I had thought I was assertive. She disrespected my tardiness and lack of organization. I thought I was a multitalented creative spirit out to touch the world.

I knew it was time to repent. If you don't humble yourself, the Lord has ways of doing it for you. My judgmental attitude had to go. The Lord began to show me His "severe mercy." He taught me to be slow to speak, careful to judge, and quick to forgive, and He made me more aware of my own need to be forgiven. The process has shown me the depths of His grace and boundless love. I have sincerely embraced the concept of being His workmanship, although I still squirm while I'm being worked on.

I now enjoy meaningful relationships with the blonde women—and many others who don't "look" like me. Our senior pastor is an African American, and the church is gloriously integrated. Our neighborhood is comprised of families whose ancestry can be traced to five continents. There is even a house with an opinionated Italian woman from New York.

Therefore, as God's chosen people, holy and dearly loved, clothe yourselves with compassion, kindness, humility, gentleness and patience. Bear with each other and forgive whatever grievances you may have against one another. Forgive as the Lord forgave you. And over all these virtues put on love, which binds them all together in perfect unity.
—Colossians 3:12-14 (NIV)

2

My Promise Keeper

h, the things you do for love. I'm talking about the real deal, not the imposters from Madison Avenue or Victoria's Secret. And not the "I love you, man!" brand. And certainly not the cheap imitations that Hollywood serves up fresh every month. I'm talking about the genuine, sacrificial, "for better or for worse," "I'll be there through the good, bad and ugly," "I commit my life to you" level of love. That kind of love is a beautiful thing.

During my senior year of college, I returned home to Long Island for Christmas vacation. Everyone had been raving about a new eatery called Tiffany's Café (Rosie O'Donnell's favorite hangout before she was famous). I called some girlfriends who were also home on break, and we went on a Saturday night to check it out. It was huge and had Victorian decor with amber lighting. Antique brass and oak pieces were positioned throughout the huge room and midcentury *Life* magazines were spread on wall-length racks around the lobby. Just inside the main room, two massive rectangular oak chests held piles of game boxes—Scrabble, Parcheesi, backgammon, chess, and checkers. In the middle of the café, a small octagonal platform rose five feet above the tables and booths. A musician was perched on a stool as he strummed his twelve-string guitar and crooned the best of Simon and Garfunkel, James Taylor, Seals and Croft, Carol King, and Bread. We had a delightful evening, and I wondered who had the sensitivity, insight, and creativity to birth such a place.

As we paid the bill, I inquired about the restaurant, and my friends "dared" me to audition to sing there one night. I had only sung and played guitar in church, so at my Tiffany's debut, I mixed love songs about guys with love songs about God.Amy Grant, Chuck Girard, Second Chapter of Acts, Chris Christian, Michelle Pillar— great songs. Well, I thought they were great. Nobody seemed to be listening except for my grinning friends and the male cashier. I later learned he was the owner. You'll never guess his name. Four years later, I met him at the altar.

Frank and I will celebrate our twentieth anniversary next year, and we have actually gotten a handle on this business of love. Don't misunderstand. I've loved Frank since that talk on the park bench at Northport Harbor. In hindsight, what I felt for my future mate was kid stuff, not very unlike what I felt for Steven Zelinski in fifth grade. My love for both Steven and Frank had more to do with how they made me feel and what emotional benefits I received, rather than what I was capable of offering. Steven got my baseball-card collection, and Frank got my hand in marriage. Steven got a full box, and Frank got a mixed bag.

Our first year of marriage was blissful. We both worked full-time during the day and pursued graduate courses at night. My classes were Tuesdays and Thursdays, and his were Mondays and Wednesdays. We met for dinner at dozens of restaurants between SUNY Stony Brook and C.W. Post, and once in a while, Frank would bring a cassette tape of our wedding song and ask the manager to pop it into the sound system. We watched a fairly new program called *Nightline* most evenings and occasionally had milk and Oreos in bed. The weekends were all ours, and we occasionally headed to Boston, the Berkshires, or the Hamptons. Year two was more of the same. We completed our respective masters' degrees, took a life-changing missions trip to Haiti, and had a crash course in mourning when Frank's father died of a sudden, massive heart attack.

Somewhere between years three and five, the novelty and purity of "Yes, honey—Sure, honey—No problem, honey—

Whatever you decide, honey" wore off and was replaced with "Why do you do that?—Don't touch my stuff!—Go ahead, but I'm not involved—What do you expect?" I started making piles, and Frank started discarding my piles. I was busy bonding with people, and Frank began creating lists and priorities (for me). I began to dabble in the kitchen, and Frank started charting everything from personal goals to personal prayer to personal finances—MY personal finances! He discovered the Day-Timer and decided the whole world should have one. Since then, he has never been seen without it. It's his constant companion and brings him more comfort than I care to discuss.

Years six through ten of our marriage are kind of blurry. I realize now it was an extended case of sleep deprivation. Actually, what I do remember most clearly about those years is the fluid. Lots of fluid. Little sleep. Frank bought a small manufacturing plant, attended law school every night, and became Chairman of the Board for Long Island Youth for Christ. While Mr. Wonderful built up his intellectual, psychological, and spiritual muscles, I put on over forty pounds in order to bear him a child. Four years later, we had three little Lofaros in all. Those generational sins started "visiting" us (So that's what that passage meant!). Virtues and vices surfaced in our little ones and in our marriage. Needless to say, the trials, challenges, and struggles caused all kinds of new "baggage" to appear. It was heavy and did not always smell sweet.

The next few years were full of upheaval, transition, and adjustment, and yet, it was a strangely calming time in our marriage. Frank's decision to enter full-time Christian work made an enormous impact on our lives. A move out of state caused us to renew and rediscover our friendship with one another. (If possible, try this without leaving the state.) Our parenting skills improved and so did our ability to disagree in an agreeable manner. We learned how to fight fairly and to be gentler with one another's deficits. He no longer throws my piles away; instead he just moves the boxes to the basement. I no longer hide his Day-Timer when he comes home late from work. He has lost some hair, and I have lost some bone definition in the area between my neck and ankles.

Our friendship has never been stronger. Our commitment has never been deeper. Our love has never been sweeter. Praise God that my friends once dared me to sing.

So, to Frank J. Lofaro, Jr.:

Thank you for being strong enough to admit weakness.

Thank you for being a protector and provider.

Thank you for boldly confronting your baggage and for gently exposing mine.

Thank you for being a man of integrity, discipline, devotion, and prayer.

Thank you for being a caring, affectionate, instructive father to our children.

Thank you for being a real man, a "Tender Warrior," a servant of the King.

I love you, honey. You'll always be my Franklin, and I'll always be your Eleanor.

*A*bove all, love each other deeply, because love covers over a multitude of sins.

—1 Peter 4:8 (NIV)

3

Rules of the Game

ack in ancient times before I had children (B.C.), I frequently observed various scenarios in which knee and hip-high creatures (called children) would literally bring full-sized creatures (called parents) to their knees, to their wits' end, to utter despair—and ultimately—to surrender. Of course, all of these showdowns took place in public settings; hence, my acute analysis. By the time I was a college sophomore studying education and communication, I knew, beyond any shadow of a doubt, that these displays would never take place if I were a parent. Never.

Some of you are smirking. And I know what you're thinking. *Never say never, Ellie. Tell the rest of your story and spare the lies. Please don't tell us your children are perfect. We'll gag.* Okay, okay—I *will* tell the story, and it'll be nothing but the truth. Our first child *was* perfect. How could theologians suggest that humans are born with sin natures? Preposterous! She was kind, affectionate, sweet, considerate, obedient, cooperative, and honest. She really was perfect! Then she turned eighteen . . . (months).

It was a Tuesday afternoon in January. I gave her a simple directive concerning the touching of something fragile. She shook her head left to right. I repeated my request and she blurted an adamant, "No!" I gave clear instructions one more time, and she shook her head, her arms, and her torso and screeched out "No!"

three times in a row. I shot back "Yes!" three times and removed the object from the table. The little, red-faced cherub dropped to the den carpet and cried herself to sleep. *Mother: One. Child: Zero.*

A few days later, we were in the checkout line at the supermarket. Every aisle had a line three or four carts deep. My cart was overflowing, and there were even groceries stuffed up against my perfect child. (I had attributed the outburst earlier in the week to gastrointestinal discomfort.) I approached the conveyor belt and began the robotic task of emptying the cart I had just taken an hour to fill. Sixty seconds later, a few of the people in my vicinity started chuckling. I turned around to find the little cherub wildly consuming a bag of M & M's that she apparently picked up from the candy rack, which was conveniently located within a ten-inch reach.

Naturally, I chuckled with the adoring audience and told my little honey to hand me the candy. I attempted to remove the bag from those pudgy little hands, but the little hands suddenly had an iron grip. I pulled and she pulled and I pulled and the bag tore and the M & M's went flying all over the floor. The candy bounced, the cherub wailed, and the number of onlookers doubled. I tried to comfort her, but her cries grew louder and longer. The cart was still more than half full, and the ice cream was starting to thaw. I unloaded the cart at a frenzied pace, and I dropped a large jar of olives on the floor. The jar shattered, and olives rolled around and commingled with the M & M's. Have you ever smelled olive juice? The floor at my feet was shiny and gross. The baby continued to emit deafening shrills somewhat similar to an air-raid siren and refused to be comforted. The audience tripled in size. I was convinced that at any moment, an announcement would be made through the PA system: "Will the pathetic woman in aisle six please clean up her mess and control her offspring?!" I did what any other self-respecting woman would do. I ripped open a new bag of M & M's and handed it to the little darling who stopped crying instantaneously. *Child: Ten. Mother: Zero.*

Maybe there *was* some merit to the whole concept of original sin after all. I had lived through (and barely survived) our first child's first temper tantrum. I looked up "tantrums" in the Bible— nothing. (Although there was a lengthy explanation of stiff necks.)

I checked my child-psychology textbooks—a lot of mumbo jumbo about letting the little person discover her own boundaries, her own comfort zones, and her own means of expression. Parents were warned not to hinder any of this discovery for fear of damaging the child's self-esteem, which would surely land her in therapy as a young adult.

Not long after the supermarket scene, our perfect child told her first lie and stole her first cookie. Where does a two-year-old go to learn how to lie and steal? Where does a mother go to swallow her pride? How about to eat crow? My husband and I were discouraged and knew we needed a solid plan of action. I had seen the results of Dr. Spock's methods, and I knew he was not the way to go. T. Berry Brazelton was a popular child psychologist at the time, but like Benjamin Spock, he was soft on discipline and big on feelings. And we all know where feelings take us. In the late 1980s, most experts were lax about establishing and enforcing the rules of the game of life and squeamish at best about penalizing young players for infractions. Enter Dr. James Dobson.

Talk radio had become popular with the masses, and there was no shortage of it. Christian ministries realized the potential in media and not a minute too soon. A friend from church who also happened to be a "seasoned mom" told me when and where I could find the *Focus on the Family* program on the radio dial. I tuned in the very next day, and life in the Lofaro home has never been the same. Within the year, I read all his books on "bringing up children in the way they should go," and Frank and I were amazed by how wise and effective Dobson's advice proved to be. And he's not the only one out there. You can find a plethora of Christian material to improve your parenting skills: Crabb, McDowell, Smalley, Trent, Yates, Wright, McArthur—read 'em and reap!

I'm continually puzzled by the fact that people will read lengthy instructions for new televisions, stereos, and computers. Many will invest in costly manuals, which teach the reader everything from financial investments to gourmet cooking to training a pet. Aren't our children more fragile, more important, and more precious than any of the *things* we value? You know the answer.

Why then are we so hesitant to read instructions, to take a parenting course, to ask for some help? May the Lord forgive our foolish pride!

Frank and I are far from being the perfect parents, and we do not have three perfect kids. However, I am happy to report that knowledge of the things of God illuminates our paths and makes the crooked ways straight. Our baby has grown into a lovely young lady. Thanks to the wisdom of God's Word and those who have been gifted to expound upon it, we never went through the terrible twos. When Paris turned thirteen, we did not buy into secular thinking that maintains that your sweet child will turn sour during the teen years. Even the guidance office sent home an educational newsletter warning us not to worry if our teen seems suddenly aloof. I don't buy it. Am I living in a bubble? Hardly. Just following instructions.

Train up a child in the way he should go,
And when he is old he will not depart from it.
—Proverbs 22:6 (NKJV)

4

Fish Tale

When I think of outdoor sports, fishing never comes to mind. That would be understandable if I had spent my childhood in Iowa, but in fact, I grew up on an island. My parents never fished a day in their lives. I don't fish. Frank doesn't fish. The kids have never fished. Well, actually they watched a guy fish once. I am well aware that fishing at an ocean, a lake, and a stream are all quite different—I have even experienced deep-sea fishing on two occasions. I don't have pleasant memories of either one. Once, we boarded a charter vessel off the coast of Maui. I was seven months pregnant. Who knew? I still have flashbacks of fish blood, slime, eyeballs, and rocking that wouldn't cease. The other episode was off the east end of Long Island. I was better prepared. After ingesting a box of Dramamine, I slept through the four-hour excursion. Frank and two men had to carry me to the car when it was all over. It was an expensive outing—twenty-five dollars an hour to be in a coma.

Now that we live in northern Virginia, fishing seems to come up much more often. The Potomac River, the Chesapeake Bay, and numerous lakes seem to beckon young and old alike. Even some of the women fish. The children have asked to go fishing on numerous occasions, and we felt it was time to honor their request. Actually, our youngest daughter, Capri, made three wishes when she turned eight. (She has stopped wishing for a puppy—at least out loud—thank you, Jesus.) She wanted to climb a mountain, to milk a cow, and to go fishing before the start of third grade. What a sweetie. How could we let her down? Summer was coming to an end, and it seemed like we were about to do just that. I tried to create some guilt in Frank, and he reminded me that he was in favor of the puppy. If Capri's three wishes were to be granted, *I* was going to have to become proactive. This is our baby—the last to be born—the one with no baby album—the one we never read to—the one who wears all hand-me-downs. Granting at least *one* of her birthday wishes became my goal in life.

I had heard about Deep Creek Lake, nestled in the Allegheny Mountains at the westernmost tip of Maryland. Pittsburgh is two hours north, Ohio is four hours west, and West Virginia is twenty minutes to the south. After some research, I discovered that it was just a three-hour drive from our home, not too far for a three-day, end-of-summer romp. We arrived at night, so there wasn't much to see. We went to dinner at "the best Italian restaurant on the lake." I'll say no more about that.

The next morning, the kids awoke early and ran down three long flights of wooden steps to the dock of the condo complex. Twenty minutes later, Capri was the first to reach the side of my bed. Breathless and bursting with excitement, she pleaded for me to get up, get dressed, and get down to the lake ASAP. Two hours later, we were all dressed, fed, and standing inside Johnny's Bait and Tackle Store. Johnny and his wife Ethel have been there since God created fish. We rented three rods, one per child, and bought a bucket of live minnows. Johnny advised us never to buy dead ones. Back at the dock, we set up camp. Well, not an *actual* camp. We don't camp, which is linked to why we don't fish. Frank's idea of "roughing it" is a Marriott without twenty-four-hour room service. You can take the New Yorker out of New York, but . . .

Frank gave the kids a three-minute casting class, and the moment of truth finally arrived. Who was going to spear the eyes, brains, and guts of the first, cute, little, helpless baby minnow? Not I. Not my innocent children. All human (and minnow) eyes were on Frank. He showed no enthusiasm, so I reminded him of his priesthood, and he proceeded to cold-bloodedly bait the first hook. Paris groaned, Capri looked away, and Jordan got misty. I informed them the minnow never knew what hit him and they believed me for an entire ten seconds, at which point in time the poor thing wriggled off the hook and did back flips on the dock. He back flipped his way right off the edge of the dock and into the lake and the children cheered. Somehow, we were caught in a surreal version of *Free Willy.* Same theme—much smaller fish. Frank reached into the bucket and Mr. Minnow number two did not have the same good fortune as number one. It took forty minutes for three lines to be baited, cast, and settled upon the lake.

If you think there's a lot of time between pitches in baseball—ya ain't seen nothin'. Fishing is a waiting game. Enthusiasts claim it's mostly mental, and I will have to concur. It's definitely mental. Only the fish were successful at fishing—in less than two hours, twenty-two minnows had lost their lives. I can just imagine the conversation down below.

"Hey guys—over here! The fools from New York are serving free sushi."

"It's all you can eat. Come and get it!"

I had a feeling Frank's baiting technique needed major adjustments, so I gingerly suggested he spend some time at Johnny's. We were about to call it a day when suddenly Capri's rod began to bend. And bend. And bend. She squealed with delight as Frank helped her to reel in her catch. She never took her hand off the rod, and before we knew it, Capri was holding a three-foot fish. Okay—it was actually ten inches but it looked like three feet next to her compact, four-foot frame. Frank unhooked the fish and returned it to the lake. Capri was beaming.

The next day, we dressed in swimsuits, packed a deli lunch, bought a tube, and headed to Bill's Marina where we rented a motorboat for the afternoon. Frank was given two-minute driving instructions (didn't you have to take a two-day course at one time?), and we were suddenly revving away from the marina. Deep Creek Lake is twelve miles long, and we were determined to see it all. Jordan was the first volunteer to be pulled in the tube, and when we picked up speed, the tube picked up water and Jordan disappeared.

When he surfaced, he was screaming at the top of his lungs, claiming the fish were eating him. It was actually the towrope wrapped around his legs. He was eventually consoled. Paris and Capri followed, and before we returned the boat, yours truly took a turn. Frank decided to pick up speed as I held on to the tube and prayed. I wondered about the kids' love for me as they begged Frank to go full throttle.

That night, the Annual Garrett County Agricultural Fair came to life, and the Lofaro family experienced a lot of firsts. There were varied contests—calf tying, sheep shearing, and to our amazement . . . cow milking! Capri's eyes filled with delight. Scores of young people involved in 4-H Clubs showed off everything from milk-fed lambs to corn bread. Capri milked a cow after receiving some guidance from a kind Amish farmer. The next morning, we took a hike up a mountain named Wisp. The children slept soundly as we drove home that night, and Frank and I smiled and gave thanks as we considered the goodness of the Lord.

Isn't it amazing that God can hear the yearnings of an eight-year-old? He also hears the eighty-year-old and the newborn. The Word tells us He takes pleasure in granting the desires of our hearts. What do you desire this day? Ask. Seek. Knock. Our Father in heaven longs to give good gifts. Are your hands open? Is your heart expectant? Are you looking in His direction? His hands were pierced and His heart was broken as He was looking in yours.

Delight yourself in the Lord
and he will give you the desires of your heart.
—Psalm 37:4 (NIV)

5

The Summer of '96

As the leaves begin to turn and the night air begins to bring a slight chill, I still feel warm when I reflect on so many wonderful summer memories. I will never forget the summer of 1996. In June, the whole family spent two weeks on the ocean in Duck, North Carolina. We loved it there. In July, the kids and I went to New York and spent two weeks visiting family and friends. We ate our way from home to home, and when we weren't being hosted, we bought pizza by the slice and Carvel ice cream. In August, we spent most days at the local town pool where the little ones were quite content to swim all day, and I was quite content to catch up on good reading. Like millions of other Americans, we also spent a fair amount of time watching television that summer.

The world spotlight beamed on Atlanta, where the Olympians struggled for victory and agonized over defeat. The children had a good dose of athletics and then a taste of political science with the party conventions in San Diego and Chicago. Frank and I were very impressed by their level of interest. After all, the conventions were much more focused on "family values" than they had been in the past. There were movie stars, singers, war heroes, and videos of the candidates' childhood homes, and I'll not soon forget the speeches by J. C. Watts and Elizabeth Dole.

I just loved when she walked out to the conventioneers. The whole family was entertained.

Then came the other media-saturated event of the summer: the explosion of TWA Flight 800. On the night of July 17, I kissed Paris, Jordan, and Capri and tucked them into the guest room beds of my mother-in-law's home in eastern Long Island. After prayers and drinks of water and hugs and more water, I returned to the den to find Frank's mother with her hands over her mouth. We watched the burning fuselage until 2 am We heard distant sirens into the early morning. We returned to CNN when we awoke, but this time, the children were not welcomed to the room with the TV. I could not formulate a coherent lesson to impart. I could not transform it into a teachable moment. I felt only a deep ache, which grew in the days to follow. Numbers became names. Names became faces. Faces became people who were deeply loved. Thousands of lives were changed forever.

The next night, I explained to the children that a terrible thing happened to a plane and many people had died. I refrained from any commentary or theorizing about the cause. My explanation was brief, disjointed, and similar to the title of a book written by a Rabbi, "Sometimes bad things happen to good people." Only our nine-year-old was interested in knowing more. She seemed fairly satisfied after a ten-minute exchange. I reminded her that each day is a gift from God and only He knows how long we will live on the earth. I also added a brief, seemingly inadequate definition of eternity. Children often understand much more than we give them credit for.

A week later, Frank flew up to Long Island to join us for three days. It's amazing how a catastrophe gets our attention and reminds us of our priorities. Frank travels extensively for Prison Fellowship International, so when he landed in New York, he got more hugs and kisses than he ever anticipated. It was a sweet reunion; we were happy to all be together again. The following morning, we put on bathing suits, packed a lunch and headed to the ocean at Robert Moses Park. A favorite CD was playing, the sky was bright blue, the sun was shining, the windows were down, and we were singing and laughing and recounting details of our week to Frank. Traffic on the Long Island Expressway was unusually heavy for a Saturday morning, and before we could get to Exit 53 South, the cars merged into a single lane and came to a complete stop. We wondered if it was roadwork or maybe an accident. What we saw silenced our complaints.

As we inched forward, we realized that traffic was halted so that a special envoy of state and federal vehicles could escort a massive crane down the two left lanes of the expressway heading toward eastern Long Island. It was covered in the green hues of military camouflage and looked powerful enough to easily pull a combat tank out of desert sand. Frank and I knew immediately where that crane was going and what it would be used for. I turned the music off and he raised the windows and we asked the children to be quiet for a little while. We glanced at one another and communicated clearly without words. There were moms and dads and sisters and brothers and daughters and sons whose lives were senselessly cut short—whose bodies were strewn on an ocean floor—whose tomorrows would never come.

I thought about the couple who were going on their honeymoon to Paris and remembered how Frank and I did the very same thing fourteen summers earlier. I thought about the young flight attendant taking her first transAtlantic shift and pondered how proud her family must have been of this "promotion." I thought about the students from Pennsylvania and wondered what I would do if one of my children were aboard.

We drove another fifty yards, and I thought about the explosion in the Olympic Centennial Park and the one in Oklahoma City and the one in the World Trade Center. My heart sank a bit, my stomach tightened a bit, and my fear grew a bit. I felt a mixture of anger and sorrow about the world my children are growing up in. I felt some despair as I considered that America is no longer exempt from acts of terrorism. It was a helpless feeling. The presence of the crane alongside cars filled with kids, chairs, and beach balls created an emotional juxtaposition too complex for words.

We finally broke from the crawling line and headed south on the Sagtikos Parkway. As we neared the Robert Moses Causeway, my then four-year-old daughter Capri leaned forward and tapped my shoulder.

"Mommy, if you love Jesus, you never have to die."

The teachable moment concerning TWA Flight 800 had finally come.

Fortunately, I was listening.

I assure you, those who listen to my message and believe in God who sent me have eternal life. They will never be condemned for their sins, but they have already passed from death into life.

—John 5:24 (NLT)

6

Be at the Gate

ainy days and Mondays don't always get me down, but they
sure make me sleepy. Especially when the rainy day is a
gloomy, chilly Monday in late fall. The laundry was folded and
put away. The kitchen floor was mopped erasing the evidence of
heavy weekend traffic. The guest bedroom sheets were changed.
The Bible study that I teach was prepared, and the homework
for the Bible study that I attend was completed so, at 3:45 on that
particular November afternoon, I plopped on the couch with a
Time magazine. I knew the house would come alive with dramatic
stories, snacks, homework, permission slips and the like at 4:02, as
it does every weekday. Lord, let these seventeen minutes stretch in
a supernatural way. As a matter of fact, please stop the time, Lord.
You've done it before. I really need a good naaa . . .

Raindrops rolled down the den windows. The wind
blew. Branches swayed, and the leaves fell. The house let out an
occasional creak. I read two lines and fell fast asleep. I was down for
the count. As you may have guessed, the Lord did not answer my
prayer. After what felt like a minute, the front door flew open with
an announcement from our gregarious son Jordan. "Maaaaaaa! We're
ho-o-ome!" I can always count on the little guy for a bear hug. My
daughter Paris had become a sophisticated preadolescent. She came
to the outer rim of my personal space and whispered, "Hello,

Mother," without making eye contact. Following closely behind, as is her lot in life, was my baby. Capri had finally turned six after what seemed like an eternity of being stuck at five and a half.

Along with energizing me and bringing our home much joy and laughter, Capri makes me even more tired than rainy days and Mondays. She knows what she wants and when she wants it. She doesn't let the big kids pull anything over on her. She chooses items at the supermarket and places them in the cart. (The older two would NEVER have tried this.) She refuses to kiss friends and relatives on command. She is the one with a heavy Brooklyn accent even though we moved from New York when she was two. And with that accent, she tells people what she thinks of them and how they smell. This is the child who has me rereading Dobson's bestsellers. That particular day was like all others in that she dropped her coat in the foyer, her backpack in the entrance of the den, and her well-guarded, handheld artwork on the coffee table. She shunned her big girl persona and reverted to playing baby of the house. "Mommy, Mommy, I missed you, Mommy." Her thumb went into her mouth and she climbed on top of me. We cuddled for a blissful moment. Her thumb got a brief reprieve.

"Mommy, I do not like dis weathuh."

"Me neither."

"Are you sick or sumthin?"

"No, Mommy's just a little tired."

"Did you exacise or sumthin?"

"No, I'm too old to exercise."

"How old are you anyway?"

"I'm thirty years old."

"No yaw not! Yaw fawty-one! Fakuh!"

"If you know my age, why did you ask?"

"I was just checkin' ta see if you know."

"Mommies know a lot of things."

"Will you be dead for my wedding?"

"No, I plan to be there. Daddy might be dead. He's older than me."

"How old will you be when I'm fawty?

"I'll be seventy-five."

"How old will you be when I'm fifteen?"

"I'll be fifty." (ouch)

"How will I find you when I get ta heaven?"

"I'll be in the Italian restaurant at the all-you-can-eat buffet."

"Mommy. I'm sewious."

"Oh, honey, you won't have to worry about that. Jesus will show you where I am."

"How does God put people in hell? Does He drop 'em in?"

"Well, no. It's kind of hard to explain, but you don't need to worry, because you're going to heaven."

"Does God have a list of who's goin' ta heaven?"

"Yes, as a matter of fact He does."

"What if yaw on the list and do a bad thing?"

I glanced over at the magazine and wanted to suggest she could ask the person on the cover, but I caught myself and remembered she was only six. "If you are really sorry for your sin, God can see into your heart and He will forgive you. The thief on the cross didn't act very nice, and he did a lot of bad things, but he is in heaven because he was very, very sorry and he believed in Jesus."

"Do we have ta brush teeth in heaven?"

"No, we'll all have dentures that don't wear out."

"Do we have ta take showuhs?"

"Nope. Everybody there smells good forever."

"I'm gonna like heaven. Just make shaw yaw right there when I get there." She poked her tiny pointer finger close to my nose and said with rhythm, authority, and a semithreatening tone, "Be at da gate and don't be late! You got it?"

I pulled her forty-pound frame closer toward me and held her tight. "I got it."

Homework time and dinner time and bath time and devotion time and tuck-in time all came and went on that rainy Monday night. As I laid my own body down to sleep, I thought about heaven and how far away it seems. I thought about the people whom I love who have found their eternal rest. I thought of those who look for rest everywhere except in God. I'm told eternity is a very long time and that heaven is a very wonderful place. My deepest desire for my family, my friends, and my neighbors isn't really any different than that of a six-year-old. Be at the gate and don't be late. It's a finish line you'll want to be sure to cross.

⨍don't know about you, but I'm running hard for the finish line. I'm giving it everything I've got. No sloppy living for me!

—1 Corinthians 9:26 (*The Message*)

7

Free 9 to 3

The pencils were sharpened, the backpacks zipped, the nylon lunch bags filled, and my three precious children looked quite adorable in their brand-new school outfits. After a sumptuous serving of pancakes and sausage (it was the last hot breakfast they got until Thanksgiving), it was time to brush teeth, tie shoelaces tightly, and take some pictures out on the driveway (because the morning grass was too wet). "Cheeeeeeeez!"

Our ten-year-old daughter was beginning fifth grade, our eight-year-old son third, and our baby girl in full-day kindergarten. That particular first day of school was like no other. It deeply affected my life. It was momentous. It rearranged my priorities. It gave me new options. In short, it changed everything. That particular first day of school involved all three children attending school all day for all seven hours. For the first time in ten years, I would have the luxury of "free" time—a lot of free time.

I dropped Paris and Jordan off in the designated spot of the car-pool lot and swung around to another building to park and walk Capri to her new classroom. The kindergartners were located in portables that had decklike ramps and railings leading up to them. There were many moms, a few dads, and dozens of little five-year olds along the ramp waiting for the teachers to open the classroom doors. Some kids were crying, and some were on the verge, and some mothers looked teary eyed. Obviously, these were the freshmen moms. It was easy to pick them out. They were the ones toting around video cameras, Beanie Babies, and human babies. This was a first for many of them. They were the ones who lingered and chatted nervously about backpacks and healthy snacks. They performed jumping jacks and sent love messages with exaggerated gestures through the classroom windows after their children were allowed inside.

Not I. You see, I was a senior mom. I had been at it ten years already. I knew that a healthy snack was a cookie without chocolate. I stopped taking video footage after the third child's first birthday party. I don't carry around Beanie Babies—never even bought one. (Don't be concerned; we now have two dozen Beanies in the house from people who felt sympathetic.) I hugged little Capri, told her to suck it up, and promised her money if she didn't cry. We haggled for a minute and settled on an amount.

I headed back down the ramp with a lilt in my step and was about to get into the Volvo when I looked to my left and saw a young freshman mother slouched over her steering wheel with a tear-drenched face. I tapped on her passenger window and she lowered it while wiping her cheeks. I stuck my head in to see if she was okay. We chatted for a while. I shared a few words of wisdom, uttered a quick but sincere prayer, and advised her to study a second language, enroll in a book club, take up archery, or join a health club. She thanked me for my encouragement and said she had to go home to clean the house.

As I pulled away from the school lot that day, my head was swirling with the choices and possibilities that would await me in the coming months. I would have more time for reading and writing. I would be better prepared to speak at the two upcoming women's retreats. I would now have a lot more time to do thorough cross-referencing and etymological searches in the Pentateuch for the weekly class I was attending. I could more readily entertain angels unaware and take more meals to people facing a crisis. I could take a cooking class for my own meal crisis. I could send more "Thinking of you" cards, and I could finally lose those twenty pounds at the gym. I could "do lunch"!

I pulled into the garage, picked up the paper and sat at the kitchen table for a little while. The phone rang.

"Hey, honey, it's me. How did it go with the kids this morning?"

"Great. They all seemed pretty excited. Capri was a little apprehensive."

"Did she cry?"

"No way. She was fine, a real trooper—and a very good businesswoman."

"What does that mean?"

"I'll explain tonight."

"So El—what are you doing today?"

"Worried about me, Frank?"

"No, just curious. I don't want you to be bored with all this time on your hands."

"I'll try to challenge myself."

"Listen, honey, could you do some laundry today? I'm out of clean underwear. Also, my suits are ready at the dry cleaner, we need stamps, and I really need you to take that stuff back to Home Depot for a refund. And maybe you could get around to sorting through some of your piles."

"Will that be all, Master?"

"Well, since you asked, go ahead and throw together one of your tasty but simple meals for tonight. Moffitt, Javier, and Ivan are in the country for meetings all week, and I hate to see them stuck in the hotel every night."

"It's been so nice to hear from you Frank."

"Love you—you're the best!"

"Thank you, honey. Call any time."

As I hung up the phone that morning, my focus abruptly shifted from desires to duties. Our culture does not encourage me to put my desires aside in order to serve the needs of others. On the contrary, I am bombarded with both subtle and overt reminders to make myself a priority. In her magazine O, Ms. Winfrey regularly encourages women to do only what they want to do. After all, who will look out for you if you don't look out for yourself?

For the Christian woman, young or old—married or single—the answer is Jesus. Jesus will "look out" for you. Jesus will promote you. Jesus will enlighten you. Jesus will protect you. Jesus will improve you. And when you're called to serve a crying child, a moody teenager, a tired husband, or a difficult employer—it's Jesus who will come alongside and help you do all things well. He was the greatest servant of all and He makes the journey a joyful one, no matter what we face along the way.

Work hard and cheerfully at whatever you do, as though you were working for the Lord rather than for people. Remember that the Lord will give you an inheritance as your reward, and the Master you are serving is Christ.

—Colossians 3:23-24 (NLT)

8

Resolutions

o there I was, sitting in a friend's living room with a group of women during the holiday season, and before I knew it, we were onto the subject of New Year's resolutions. "Isn't that a worldly concept?" one woman asked. "Not really," quipped another. "You can resolve to do all kinds of wonderful things. Read *The One Year Bible,* take a class, become more organized, baby-sit for young mothers, go for a mammogram, fast more often for your own children." I got up to get another cannoli.

Not many cannolis in Virginia, and besides, the men were in the kitchen discussing the national debt, a personally less threatening subject than the one going on in the living room. I shared my impressions of Alan Greenspan and was then beckoned back to the living room. "Do you exercise, Ellie?" an unfamiliar thin woman asked in front of the group. *What did she mean?* Mothering and marriage and laundry and cleaning and carpooling and mopping up after the kids' vomit! Of course I exercise! How kind of her to clarify with, "I'm speaking of regularly scheduled, focused exercise." I told her I was a great field hockey player just twenty years ago. She laughed . . . and persisted. "Surveys show that if a person does not have an exercise regiment by age forty, he or she will most likely never begin." *Great,* I thought to myself. *I don't even have to think about it for a few more months.* I reached for the dip as she nibbled on plain celery.

"Do YOU exercise?" I retorted.

"Oh yes, an hour a day. Our bodies are the temple of the Holy Spirit." If she's a temple, then I'm a town.

"I suppose you also count your fat intake . . ." was my next effort at civility.

She grinned proudly. "Well, actually, I'm on a practically fat-free diet." Of course. As the group discussion continued, I learned that the "thin" woman was another guest's sister visiting from out of state. Her husband is a health fanatic, they're wealthy, and she never had children. I felt strangely avenged.

Poor thing. She probably spends so much time at the spa because she's lonely. Her December tan became more obvious. I felt pity for her. She'll never know the joy of stretch marks.

Let's face it. We all know very thin people are usually obsessive and unhappy. Have you ever known a "jolly" skinny person? My neighbor runs thirty miles a week, and her face seems to be sagging prematurely. That famous marathon runner in Boston died while he was running! And do not forget the matters of shin-splints, pulled ligaments, sprained ankles, and avoiding unleashed dogs. Those who work at being thin indoors are also at serious risk. I have a friend who smashed her left arm while she did a slide move in aerobics class. She is healing steadily, but in the meantime, she has four steel surgical pins holding her bone to her flesh. I've always known that vigorous exercise is potentially hazardous to one's health. "Any more dip?"

The conversation in the living room turned toward our various "resolutions" to devote more time to studying the Word, while the men shifted to Super Bowl jabber. (The kitchen certainly had more laughter than the living room.) A young mother opened her heart, "I really struggle to find the time to read, or sometimes, even to pray with four children all under the age of six."

An experienced mom with kids in college responded in a loving but firm manner, "Oh no, dear—you must make your time with God your highest priority. If you are not on track with the Lord, every circumstance will derail you." The other mothers had the look of "train wreck" suddenly written all over their faces (myself included). I attempted to bring some comfort, so I reminded the ladies of His wonderful grace, mercy, strength, and provision. Another friend encouraged us to grasp the fact that Jesus loves us fully, unconditionally, and without regard to our response or performance.

Miss Twiggy piped up. "Actually, I have a great suggestion for studying the entire Bible in one year. Anyone with desire and a little time each day could do it." *A little time.* Isn't that what each mother would give her left thigh for? Isn't that the real problem here? Isn't this fitness-club fanatic out of touch? I assumed she found some free time between the boutique, the club, and the tanning bed. Lord, please send me some agape right away!

My curiosity was piqued. "Please tell us how you accomplished such a wonderful goal. Maybe we can all benefit."

She smiled broadly and sat up straighter (looking even thinner!), cranberry punch in hand. "Well, Harry and I decided to invest in the deluxe edition of the fully narrated *New King James Version* of the entire Old and New Testaments. It has complete sound effects and professional actors, so the Word really comes to life!" How nice for her. The Word really comes to life for me on the days when I still love Frank and the children at sundown.

The hostess graciously asked Ms. LaLanne what time of day she suggested one listen to the tapes if one had the time to do so. Once again, she sat up straight, "Our Father in Heaven wants us to make every moment count. Our minutes are like coins, spent once and gone forever." I suddenly realized I had thrown away thousands of dollars through the years doing bathroom and kitchen floors. Probably thousands more in the laundry room. A burst of loud laughter erupted from the kitchen. Jane Fonda continued. "I pop the tapes into my Walkman and listen for an hour a day at the spa. Time on the treadmill and StairMaster flies by more quickly, and I get blessed! On all levels!"

Suddenly a ringing emanated from the corner of the room, and we realized in an instant that it was the thin woman's cellular phone. Harry had finished his late dinner meeting and needed to be picked up, and she had the rental car. In a flurry, she giggled, waved good-bye, hugged her sister, and was gone. Deep laughter erupted from our full-figured frames—directed at ourselves as much as at our thin friend. Her physical perfection had worn us out. The energy of her convictions had worn us down. And the kitchen grew very quiet as the men discussed hair loss.

*D*o nothing out of selfish ambition or vain conceit, but in humility consider others better than your-selves. Each of you should look not only to your own interests, but also to the interests of others. Your atti-tude should be the same as that of Christ Jesus.
—Philippians 2:3-5 (NIV)

9

Bumper-Sticker Wisdom

I love summertime. I love the beach, the barbecues, the birthday parties, and the ladybugs. I love staying up late and sleeping in late. I love the softball games, the ice cream cones, the warm nights, and the local pool. I love the fireworks, the wedding bells, the picnics, and the open-air concerts. I love getting to that book, catching up with that friend, finishing that project, and tossing that huge salad. Now that my "hometown" is out of state, I even love long car rides. They promise silly songs, word games, meaningful talks (with myself), great music, and bumper-sticker analysis.

Have you ever participated in the latter activity? It's hard to avoid, actually. Bumper stickers are everywhere, and they plan to stay. Does anyone know their origin, when and where the first clever phrase was adhered to the first car bumper? I would bet the mortgage payment that they caught on in that calm, deeply philosophical period known as the sixties. (WAR IS NOT HEALTHY FOR CHILDREN AND OTHER LIVING THINGS—GIVE PEACE A CHANCE—MAKE LOVE NOT WAR.) At that time, bumper stickers usually communicated something of importance about the driver's belief system. Thirty years later, that remains true for some. But nowadays, humor, satire, cynicism, frivolity, and vulgarity permeate those four-by-twelve-inch telegrams that travel the asphalt jungle.

Most bumper stickers are actually just mini-billboards touting everything from schools to restaurants to vacation spots to churches. The second most common category has to do with political races. I always admire people who keep the name of the defeated candidate on their car long after the election. Some even turn their loss into righteous indignation—DON'T BLAME ME, I VOTED FOR BUSH. The most crowded bumpers belong to people who are immersed in local politics. They have the names of the councilman, the assemblyman, the congressman, the mayor, the school-board chairman, the sheriff, the PTA president, the county clerk, the town tax collector, the library director, and the cafeteria lady plastered all over the backs of their cars. I used to think these folks had too much time on their hands, but I have come to appreciate and admire them for their commitment to grassroots politics and for keeping an eye on town hall.

My pastor once exhorted the congregation to never apologize for expressing a Judeo-Christian perspective, no matter the subject. He reminded us that our secular society does a great job of sending messages each and every day. Madison Avenue excels at that. There is no question that we are being bombarded with slogans, slants, and spins that are far from that which is good, pure, excellent, and above reproach. This may be called the Information Age, but it will also be remembered as the Indoctrination Age. So much of what comes across the radio, television, CD player, print media, and yes—even bumper stickers—rails against everything we embrace because of our devotion to the Lord. As we hear about and think about our Christian worldview and the cultural relevance of religion, we have to ask ourselves if we have a ready answer on the issues of the day. Let's take a look at some of these bumper stickers and my response to each one. Some bumper stickers make me laugh, some make me sad, and some make me downright mad.

MY CHILD IS AN HONOR STUDENT
AT JEFFERSON MIDDLE SCHOOL
*My child is working out her salvation with fear
and trembling.*

HE WHO DIES WITH THE MOST TOYS WINS
He who dies with the most toys still dies.

LIFE IS A RAT RACE
The only problem with winning the rat race is that you're still a rat.

MINDS ARE LIKE PARACHUTES,
THEY ONLY FUNCTION WHEN OPEN
When a mind is too open, the brains will spill out.

I'M THE NRA AND I VOTE
I'm NOT the NRA and I also vote (sorry, Mr. Heston).

PRO CHILD, PRO FAMILY, PRO CHOICE
Try explaining that to God.

PEACE THROUGH MUSIC
Not everybody plays an instrument.

SAVE THE BABY WHALES
What about the baby humans?

EVERY FAMILY IS DYSFUNCTIONAL—GET OVER IT
*Jesus came to bind up the brokenhearted.
He makes all things new.*

HATRED IS NOT A FAMILY VALUE
Neither is sin. (But remember to love the sinner!)

VISUALIZE WORLD PEACE
Know God, Know Peace; No God, No Peace

BASKETBALL IS LIFE, THE REST IS DETAILS
*Jesus Christ is the way, the truth, and the life.
Without Him, you can have no rest.*

MY OTHER CAR IS A BROOM
A virtuous woman, who can find (Proverbs 31)?

I SUPPORT A WOMAN'S RIGHT TO CHOOSE
One particular choice will haunt her.

COMMIT RANDOM ACTS OF KINDNESS
AND SENSELESS ACTS OF BEAUTY
*This is not an original concept.
Reread the Sermon on the Mount.*

A GOOD PLANET IS HARD TO FIND
God was obviously aware of that when
He sent His only Son.

TREES ARE THE ANSWER
Wrong!!!

Whether it's ecology, biology, sociology, or astrology—the answers to *all* the questions can only be found in a mighty triune God. Seek Him. Follow Him. Know Him. Adore Him. And when the world sends you messages of doom and gloom or elusive solutions, you can proclaim the uncompromised, unchanging, undeniable truth of God's Word. The cynics believe that LIFE S - - - - S—AND THEN YOU DIE. Wrong again. Just think of the Good News we have for them!

*L*ove does not delight in evil but rejoices with the truth.

—1 Corinthians 13:6 (NIV)

10

Confessions

I do not wish to own a pet. I do not appreciate the pet lovers who insist that a home is incomplete without a four-legged creature. Let's face it; animals were never intended to live with people. God didn't ask Noah to reside with the animals—just to give them a ride. Where else in Scripture do you see man and animal cohabiting? (No, no—the Garden doesn't count—things took a major turn for the worst after the apple episode.) There is no mention of David's dog, Esau's ferret, Mary's cat, or Joseph's goldfish. Some of Jesus' disciples were fisherman, but none of them kept the fish in the house—unless, of course, it was time to eat!

The thing that concerns me is the response I get from animal lovers when they discover we do not have a pet. Clearly, they believe my children are suffering and will not grow up to be stable, well-adjusted, productive adults. This is rather disconcerting, especially when they try to offer little tidbits of sympathy to my children.

"Maybe your mom will let you have a dog sometime soon."

"If you ever need to feel special, come on over and play with ours."

"Tell your mom that a pet will teach you how to handle responsibility."

"No, he doesn't shed, and we all feel much safer with a dog his size."

"Your mom probably had a bad experience when she was little. Pray for her."

Who are they kidding? It's the mommy and daddy who walk the thing at dusk and dawn and in bad weather. The mommy and daddy also have to change the litter and pay for new furniture and replace all the carpeting, not to mention the food and vet bills. Show me a house with an animal and I'll show you people with unwanted hair. Some animals drool and some make horrendous noises, and others scratch, sniff, and lick in places I do not care to mention. Then there is the matter of ticks, worms, fleas, sores, gas, etc.

Avowed animal lovers sign their pet's name to Christmas cards and party invitations. They take family photos with their pet, and they hang a stocking for it, and they load their grocery carts with goodies for their little furry friends. I never go down aisle fourteen at the supermarket. Never. Pet mania has encroached itself in card stores, gift shops, jewelry displays, calendars, stationery, and of course, in every bookstore. I have always admired Barbara Bush, but I must admit I felt a bit concerned about old Babs when she started getting carried away with that darn cat! (Or was it a dog?) Well, either way, that book was a big success.

On a sunny Saturday afternoon in fall, my life was deeply impacted when the three little boys across the street rang the doorbell and invited my children to come over and see the adorable seven little baby guinea pigs that were born to the big hairy mother guinea pig the day before. (Evidently, my neighbor wanted me to share in the joy—AND the adoption.) What ensued in the following days was inevitable, unavoidable, and ultimately predictable. Even Frank insisted that our children needed to care for something that eats, sleeps, and poops. In hindsight, I suppose I should have paid more attention when our kids showed inordinate excitement upon receiving digital electronic pets as gifts from people who felt pity. My kindergartener was more than a bit stressed when her GigaPet died, but I explained that everything would be okay. Sure enough, that digital doggie grew wings and flew up to heaven that very same day. (I saw it with my own eyes.) We once had fish (they all died) and major fish stuff (it's all in a box in the garage). We have also had caterpillars, fireflies, and ladybugs trapped in jars, but people tell me that none of those really count as pets.

It was time for me to die to self, put my feelings aside, eat humble pie, and warmly welcome a little critter into the house. (Well, not warmly—three out of four ain't bad.) Frank took the kids shopping to Home Depot and then Pet Depot and when all was said and done, $118 had been spent on stuff for the little rodents—er, uh, I mean rascals. Two more weeks passed, and the neighbor's guinea pigs were weaned. We received two males (the hairy kind) on a Sunday afternoon after church. Our children were elated, and the "Hallelujah Chorus" was playing in the loudspeakers of their brains. Their joy was contagious, and I remember feeling a bit embarrassed about how excited they were. Still, I could not bring myself to kiss our new housemates when they were first held up to my face. After all, they were indeed part of the rat/mouse/call-the-exterminator species.

I did stipulate that we did not want a fertile female, so we received two males—brothers. One followed the other around all day, so the children decided to name them Aaron and Moses. The guinea pigs were gently placed in a high-tech Lucite playpen, which had been freshly laid with pine bedding and stocked with furniture, toys, food, and water. The playpen became a pigpen in the days to come. The cute little creatures made cute little droppings, which created not-so-cute odors. Cleaning the pen, replacing the pine bedding, removing the droppings, and shampooing Moses and Aaron became part of the weekly routine. By week four, the thrill was gone, the volunteers were unwilling, and I was forced to impose GP Patrol. Imagine if they had to be walked.

We were away for most of December, so we had to "board" Moses and Aaron. When we returned, we were all astonished by how large they had grown. Many weeks passed, and in midMarch, Aaron became lethargic and quite sickly. The children insisted we all go to the vet. It was my first visit to a veterinarian's office and hopefully my last. The waiting room experience was more than interesting. The doctor checked Aaron and reported that the problem was intestinal. He had a very slim chance of improving. I could pay for a shot to put him to sleep or for antibiotics to administer for twenty-four hours. I asked about the cost of each and did some quick math in my head, and my ten-year-old flashed an incredulous look my way. I imagined what she might say to friends some day about the time her mean mother killed her adorable guinea pig. I opted for the antibiotics.

The next morning, the kids took me downstairs before they left for school and gave explicit instructions for me to gingerly feed medicine and water to Aaron—every hour, with a dropper between his teeth, lifting his lips, while holding his jaw still. It was a long day of life. I did my best and begged Aaron not to die while he was under my watch. By dinnertime, he was taking his last laborious breaths, and the children said their good-byes. It was a very emotional scene. My three children were all visibly upset and they held a vigil for Aaron. Their tender, innocent prayers deeply moved me. They cried for their dying guinea pig, and much to my surprise—so did I.

And [Jesus] said, "Truly I tell you, unless you change and become like children, you will never enter the kingdom of heaven."
—Matthew 18:3 (NRSV)

11

J. N. I. T. I. A. L. S.

Moving away can be a very traumatic experience. Psychiatrists say it ranks on that top-five list. I have missed pizza, pastry, pasta, and other ethnic foods (the real stuff) that we easily found in New York. I have missed being one hour away from the excitement of Manhattan and twenty minutes from some of the most beautiful beaches in the world. And what I have missed most of all are the people who have been part of our daily lives—precious family and friends who witnessed our marriage, attended our baby showers, celebrated our milestones, and shared our joys and sorrows. I felt a keen sense of a loss of roots and personal history as I stepped away from everything and everyone that was familiar. I had always boldly proclaimed, "God is my all in all." I was forced to find out if that was really true.

The population in and around the nation's capital is extremely transient. Everyone is coming and going. Not too many people here have roots in the area. Many are going up the ladder but plan to leave when they get there. Few have long-term commitments to companies, churches, schools, or relationships. The three women who were starting to like me all moved away last year, thanks to their husbands' careers. One husband is a high-ranking military officer, one is a regional sales director (he was promoted due to record-breaking Prozac sales), and one is with "the agency." More about that in a moment.

I'm not sure I will ever fully adjust to our life-changing move from the suburbs of Manhattan to the suburbs of D.C. Nobody here ever calls it Washington—just D.C. As a matter of fact, using initials for just about everything from a PB&J to the ACLU is quite the norm here. Before moving, I was only familiar with the big boys: the IRS, CIA, FBI, and HUD. However, all of that has changed. Our recent attendance at a neighbor's barbecue (here, they call it "grilling") left me quite enlightened. I had finally developed a theory about the lack of transparency in some of the people here. They all work for the government. I began to realize the tremendous impact this had on my ability to bond with people, and more specifically, with the blonde women.

Frank and I began to mingle in the group on the back deck, and it took me thirty seconds to realize we knew no one except for the hosts. We were introduced to some couples, and one of the blonde women standing very close to a tall man resembling a Ken doll asked me, "What do you do?" Notice it's never "What do you think?" "What do you feel?" or "What do you believe in?" I glanced at their "Body by Jake" physiques, quickly placed my shoulder bag over my stomach, stood up straighter, shuffled my feet and said, "I'm a homemaker." Barbie smiled in pity.

"How about you two?" I asked. They looked at one another, the husband cleared his throat, leaned toward me and blurted in a hushed tone, "We're with the agency."

"Oh, that must be very interesting work. How many people are with the CIA?"

The tall fellow got a pained look on his face. Had I been inappropriate? Did I ask something top secret? It's not like I wanted to know which dictator they were about to bring down. He cleared his throat again as his wife's smile stayed in place. "I'm not sure how many staffers are with the CIA. We're not with the CIA; we're with the DIA."

CIA—DIA—SCHMEE-IA—what's the difference? Not wanting to embarrass Frank any further, I excused us, and we meandered our way into the kitchen. The hostess was busy skewing shish kebobs

with another woman we hadn't met, so we were promptly introduced. Once again, I was asked what I do. This time, I explained I
was a domestic engineer and that I used to host a radio talk show
and had a master's degree in English literature and that I write for a
New York newspaper and several national Christian publications,
and that I speak at women's conferences from coast to coast. The
hostess's friend said she was just a housewife but that her husband
was with the agency. I tried to sound a bit more on top of things.

"Oh, that's very interesting. Is he with the CIA or the DIA?"

"Neither. He's with the NSA." Frank walked away.

I headed toward the den and perched myself in a comfortable
chair and eyed a thin, soft-covered book at the end of a shelf: *United
States Government Agencies*. It was a directory with names and
phone numbers. There were no addresses and no listings of people
or job titles. I quickly looked up NSA—National Security Agency.
(Sure sounds like an awful lot of overlapping to me. How could they
have possibly kept track of Oliver North?) My curiosity grew as I
leafed through the pages. DEA—Drug Enforcement Agency. ATF—
Alcohol Tobacco and Firearms. NRO—National Reconnaissance
Office (Mission Impossible in real life). The agencies toward the
back of the directory were less ominous. NOAA—National
Oceanographic and Atmospheric Agency. EPA—Environmental
Protection Agency. EEOC, NIH, CDC, USDA, DOT, DOE, and so on.
And that's not even counting the military section.

My compassion and agape love for the people at the party
immediately increased tenfold. Poor things. They were all carrying
sensitive, life-threatening information around with them. Their job
security comes and goes depending on who lives in the White
House. They have to wear clearance badges all day, even when they
go to the bathroom. When they read the headlines, it's old news to
them. In New York, our friends had normal jobs; electrician, nurse,
lawyer, salesman, teacher, carpenter, and yes, even housewife.

I placed the book back where I found it and out of my range
of sight, I overheard a woman's voice asking, "So, what do you do
here in D.C.?"

Without hesitation, a man's voice retorted, "I'm the EVP at
PFI." The man's voice was very familiar, and as I cranked my neck to

look around the other side of the wall, Frank sent me a wink and a smile. So what if we occasionally feel like strangers in a strange land? We've got each other, three great kids, a calling on our lives, and a promise from God that we'll live forever. I suppose that makes us very GTG (grateful to God).

> ℜejoice always; pray without ceasing; in everythin give thanks; for this is God's will for you in Christ Jesus.
> —1 Thessalonians 5:16-18 (NASB)

12

A Feast for the Soul

*I*t was the third message of rejection in as many days, and as I replayed my answering machine, I wondered what it would take for somebody to say yes. "Mrs. Lofaro, this is the volunteer coordinator from the (so and so) shelter. We have all the helpers we need to serve our Thanksgiving meal this year, but thank you for your interest and have a happy Thanksgiving."

A happy Thanksgiving? How was I supposed to have a happy Thanksgiving if I couldn't find a place for my family to give thanks by serving the less fortunate? I had thought about it for months and was sure God was pleased with the idea. After all, it was about time that we got our then twelve-, ten-, and seven-year-olds into D.C. for some hands-on ministry. I had asked around and found addresses and phone numbers. I called large inner-city churches and talked to a few people from Prison Fellowship. Surely, there was a ministry out there that would be glad to use some extra helping hands.

Not exactly. We were not the kind of volunteers most of these places were looking for. One director explained to me that they could use our help on the weekends when not too many come to help (ouch). She told me that a lot of well-intentioned Christians from the suburbs only come in for the major holidays (ouch-ouch) and although that was a noble thing, they really needed help the other forty-nine weeks of the year (ouch-ouch-ouch). Hers was our fourth rejection, but I was determined to bless the needy whether or not they wanted to be blessed.

Four days before Thanksgiving, I got through to Mrs. Mary Jane Iring of the Gospel Rescue Mission on the edge of Washington's Chinatown. She and her husband (a retired orthopedic surgeon) came to the nation's capital six years before to run a residence for seventy men, and they were soon opening a home for women. Mrs. Iring's voice sounded soothing and sweet and full of Jesus' love. "Well dear, we have all the help we need this Thursday, but your family is welcome to come and sit with our guests. We're always glad for folks who are willing to converse and make our residents and walk-ins feel special." *Converse? I can converse! No problem conversing!* I assured her that the five of us were superb conversationalists and that we would be privileged to come and visit with the special guests.

Turkey Day came, and after a Frank Lofaro deluxe breakfast, we packed into the car and headed downtown. I talked about homelessness and addiction. Frank gave the kids some rules and reminded them of God's love for all people. We parked in an abandoned lot, walked a few blocks, and entered the mission. A friendly man sent us down the cinder-block staircase, and when we arrived in the basement/dining hall, four adults were joined in prayer. Frank introduced himself and me. I introduced the children. We were met with smiles and aprons and told that they had a last minute shortage of servers, so along with the four others, we were *it!* Delicious smells oozed from the kitchen, where the feast had been prepared by residents of the mission. These men were earning a certificate in restaurant-food preparation. I was unable to persuade the fellow who made the sweet potatoes to tell me his secret ingredient; it was delectable.

Frank carved, Paris and I filled plates, and two women brought the trays to the tables, where the guests had been seated by a hostess. Jordan served warm rolls, and Capri brought iced tea to people as they sat down. I was reminded of the powerful effect little children have on adults—even those who have been harried and hardened by life on the street. After one hundred or so meals were served, we hit a brief lull, and then it picked up again.

By three o'clock, things quieted down, so we said our good-byes and headed home. I felt so good about our day and pleased that we were on schedule. We planned to return home, wash up, get dressed, and then go to a fine restaurant where I had made five o'clock reservations. It would be our very first Thanksgiving meal in a restaurant, but it was a day of firsts, and I was thankful not to have to deal with preparation and cleanup. I knew a lovely evening awaited us, and I pondered the contrast of where we had just been with where we were heading.

The sky grew dark, the drizzle grew heavier, and the passengers grew sleepy. Mutiny in the Durango was about to take place. Paris groggily suggested that we stay home, Frank perked up and seconded it, and the two younger kids came alive to make it unanimous. (I later learned it was a setup.) Frank suggested we order in Chinese. Everyone agreed. I was offended. Something clicked in my brain, and it wasn't pretty. For months I had envisioned it; for weeks I had been planning. Our families were three hundred miles away, we did not have a Thanksgiving dinner waiting at home—we had reservations that were hard to get—and I had no desire to feed our children Chinese takeout on Thanksgiving!

A lengthy debate ensued. Paris insisted she could not look at turkey or stuffing ever again. Jordan informed me he had eaten five rolls and felt nauseous. Capri told me that we had already had Thanksgiving time and that the real meaning of the day was to serve others, not ourselves. Frank wore a victorious look, and I conceded. Everyone was so happy, but I felt convinced that the local news would report that I fed my family Chinese food on Thanksgiving Day. What would my mother-in-law say?

Frank dropped us off to our warm, dry, comfortable house (which looked even more inviting after our day at the shelter) and went right back out to get a family movie and dinner. Over an hour later, he returned with a movie—but no dinner. Sheepishly, he held out the video. "I went to three Chinese restaurants, but they're all closed." The fruits of my spirit had soured.

"Do you know *why* they're all closed, Frank? I'll tell you why. All the Chinese restaurants are closed because all the Chinese people in America are home celebrating Thanksgiving by eating turkey with all the trimmings! The Chinese people are NOT eating Chinese food today! It would be *weird* to eat Chinese food today! Do you get it?"

It was five o'clock; the gray skies were now black. Frank told everybody to get pajamas and sweatpants on and to settle under blankets in the basement. Thirty minutes later, he emerged from the kitchen and descended the stairs with every tasty item that he found in the fridge, freezer, and pantry. My anger melted when I saw his creative trays of finger foods and pretty hors d'oeuvres. Our fearless leader offered a prayer and then gave a little piece of deli turkey to each person (so I could say we ate turkey on Thanksgiving). The odd meal lacked a theme, but every item was quite tasty. The movie made us laugh. The Gospel Rescue Mission caused us to receive much more than we gave, and I reflected on the countless ways the gospel has rescued me. I looked around the room at the people I love most and felt very thankful. We had feasted after all.

> And the King will tell them, "I assure you, when you did it to one of the least of these my brothers and sisters, you were doing it to me!"
> —Matthew 25:40 (NLT)

13

Vultures and Doves

I was stuffing envelopes and filing papers for my second-grader's teacher. I sat outside the door in the hallway, so as not to be a distraction to my child, whose deepest desire in life (at the moment) was to be attached to my hip. It wasn't a glamorous task, but I did get to alphabetize, which brought some small comfort. A fun-loving young teacher rounded the corner, waved, and stopped to ask if I loved *The Sopranos* as much as she did.

Now, I consider myself to be "up" on things, but this time I was stumped. "Singers?" I asked.

"No! The show!"

"On PBS?"

"No! HBO!"

"Oh . . . we don't get HBO." I decided not to pontificate. "I've heard of the Three Tenors. Those guys are great."

She looked frustrated. "No, no, no! I'm talking about *The Sopranos*. It's a family. Aren't you an Italian from New York? Where have you been? I can't believe you haven't watched it. You'd love it. It's hysterical. Raw and real about a good guy in the mafia. You *have* to see it."

It was almost lunch time (when my seven-year-old would be expecting to attach) so I smiled and offered a halfhearted promise to watch *The Sopranos* sometime. I have not watched *The*

Sopranos, but I have seen a great deal of press on *The Sopranos.* I have since heard people discussing *The Sopranos.* I have noted that other networks have released Soprano-copycats. I can say with confidence that I will never watch *The Sopranos.* Close-minded? Box-headed? Tunnel-visioned? Yes and no.

Being a lover of words, imagery, metaphors, and symbolism, I always cringe when (Christian) people criticize that which they do not take the time to learn about, let alone understand. While well-known figures may not publicly (or privately) shout the praises of my Lord and Savior, I have never lumped secular musicians, authors, entertainers, millionaires, and politicians all together in the "evil empire." (Notice I didn't mention athletes—even the most crass athletes often get a special exemption from otherwise discriminating Christians.) Although celebrities may not acknowledge God, He is still the Giver of their exceptional gifts. Their lifestyles may repel us, but I believe we can still appreciate their gifts.

So why won't I watch *The Sopranos* in order to make a more informed evaluation? We can access so much information at our fingertips that it is no longer necessary to be on full-time guard duty in order to monitor what will and will not pass into our households. I have more important things to do. Many good resources can guide those of us who want to honor our Judeo-Christian values (e.g., try screenit.com).

But who's to say that what is wrong for me is wrong for you? Nobody. Unless of course, you claim to love God with all your heart, mind, and soul. If that is the case, the whole subject of entertainment and recreation gets a lot more complicated. Check your Bible. Remember the verse about not looking at certain things? How about the one that specifically tells us what we should be looking at and thinking about? You say you were caught off guard and didn't realize what that thriller was about? Shame on you for wasting your money that way. Double shame if you didn't walk out. And parents, don't be surprised if your drooping standards cause the kids' to sink as well.

When my son Jordan was ten, he went to a sleepover at a "Christian" home. The highlight? A crude Adam Sandler flick. Imagine—the liberals of Hollywood give a movie a PG-13 rating, and the conservatives of suburbia decide it's appropriate for fourth graders. When my older daughter went to a party with other middle schoolers, the birthday girl dropped *The Blair Witch Project* into the VCR. (Yes, the parents were in the house.) Paris dismissed herself to the kitchen and by doing so, gave others the courage to do the same. Our youngest child Capri knows that Brandy, Britney, and the Backstreet Boys are not her reason for living. Should we ban ALL of it? Never. I am not fond of the Dark Ages. Let's not go back there, but let's be educated. Ignorance is *not* bliss. If you have kids, take some time to watch a TV show, listen to a song, and read a chapter of a book with them. What a wonderful opportunity to discuss family values and the narrow road that leads to life.

With or without children in the house, those of us who have the conviction to emulate God must have a higher standard than the czars and slaves of pop culture. I spoke with a churchgoing dad on the soccer field, and he explained that he listens to Howard Stern every day for sheer entertainment. When I asked about his four sons embracing Howard's views some day, he told me that will be their decision to make, not his. I am saddened to see professing Christians feeding on today's trash. And who is to say it's trash? Watch where the vultures fly. Doves, on the other hand, have singularly focused vision. They only see the goal—the destination. Nowadays, plenty of people call trash "art." But true art never made anybody sick. Am I suggesting that America is looking pale? Watch the news and decide for yourself. Consider the classic, American adage (traditionally attributed to Alexis de Tocqueville), "America is great because she is good, and if America ever ceases to be good, she will cease to be great." Are we good? The prison population has exceeded two million. Children are shooting children. Pornography spreads at epidemic proportions. Abortion is still big business. Domestic violence is on the rise. The ghetto is home to millions. Drug and alcohol abuse touch every strata of society.

"But . . . God." I love those two words. Look through Scripture at seemingly impossible circumstances. When at least one person had faith, things worked toward the good. Jesus said, "Follow me." Though it sounds simple, it demands hard choices. Let us not drown in the undertow of the enemy. Only the dead fish go *with* the flow—healthy fish swim *against* the current! If our country can be restored to greatness and goodness, it must be accomplished one household at a time.

*F*inally, brothers, whatever is true, whatever is noble, whatever is right, whatever is pure, whatever is lovely, whatever is admirable—if anything is excellent or praiseworthy—think about such things.
—Philippians 4:8 (NIV)

14

Bonbons

When I retired from teaching to embrace full-time mother-hood, I promised myself that I would never become a bonbon-popping, TV-watching, mall-strolling, phone-addicted, mindless suburban housewife. Before I had children, I looked with pity upon mothers who had neither knowledge of, nor interest in, the local, national, and global issues of the day. I was forced to repent of some of those pious attitudes when I suddenly found myself living with three humans under the age of five. I experienced some memory loss, and my knowledge of vocabulary and grammar suffered a blow. (Use it or lose it.) Once a confident trainer of high school juniors in the mastery of the verbal section of the SAT college entrance exams—I had been reduced to monosyl-labic discourse for ten hours a day. "Oooooo, whaaaaaaat, yeaaaaaah, mamamamama, dadadadadada, nonononononono." When Frank came home at night, I craved adult conversation but had only enough energy to express myself in fragments, dangling participles, and exclamations. "Don't ask what I did today! Not my job. Yes, I did. No way. My father always took care of that. It smells. Your turn. I need sleep. I'm not your mother. Buy milk?" I now admit that at times I fell into semicomas, which were induced by Big Bird or Barney.

Hosting a radio talk show for two years changed all of that. That wonderful chapter of my life served as a wake-up call to face my responsibilities as a Bible-believing, God-loving, vote-casting citizen. We are all discouraged by the startling statistics concerning abortion, divorce, crime, teenage pregnancy, suicide, drug addiction, alcoholism, prostitution, pornography, and other societal ills. As society has advanced, the church has retreated from politics, education, science, media, and the arts. So why are we surprised by moral relativity, political correctness, or even human cloning? (How fitting that the new architect of humans is named Dr. Seed.) What did we expect? Just take a look at who has been running the store. Are we surprised that our society mourns the passing of a sitcom more than the disintegration of the family? Is it any wonder that the death of the princess overshadowed the passing of a little nun from Calcutta? Why did the same system that executed Karla T. decide to allow Ted K. to grow old? What can we conclude about a government that allows partial-birth abortion but spends millions to protect endangered wildlife? Of course I want the cute little animals to live, but what about the forty million cute little babies?

I strongly reject the notion that believers should not involve themselves in public forums. Pastors who will not allow current events and local issues to be discussed and brought to light from their pulpits puzzle me. Of course, the prayer room is where our efforts must begin and end, but there are an awful lot of battles to be won. David, Joshua, and Gideon didn't just pray about their enemies. They faced them. With God's help, they defeated them. In each case, righteousness prevailed, and the course of history was altered. I am saddened by the passivity of congregations that could radically change the course of events and the fabric of their communities. Take note, my friends. Many of our towns are looking a lot more like Pottersville with each passing year. We cannot let it happen! God is able, but whom will He send? Don't let warriors in your town stand alone. God has provided courageous believers who have stood in the line of fire. Do you know who they are? Do you know what they do? Have you prayed for them or assisted them in any tangible way this past year? Have you thanked them?

I am grateful to the fervent Christians who signed the Constitution. I am indebted to the artists who lovingly recreated biblical accounts on canvas and to the actors who participated in passion plays (without heat, air-conditioning, or sound systems). The world would be a duller place without the gifts of Handel, Bach, and Mozart. Imagine our loss if Pascal, Newton, and Pasteur didn't think Christians should pioneer new territory. What would become of America if the Supreme Court justices were all atheists? Why do we get so excited when a public figure or someone with resources professes faith in Jesus? Isn't it because we, like children, want the biggest and best guys on our side? We all love a winning team, but so few are willing to take the field. Christians need to be salt and light in all arenas of our societal structure. The Army tells our young people to "Be all you can be." Frank and I tell our children the same exact thing—with a slight addendum.

When our children were all in elementary school, I asked the Lord to show me ways I could creatively and responsibly include them in the active process of good citizenship in our neighborhood and community. Living near the nation's capital causes us to feel a bit more connected to the political scene. Northern Virginia has the population of the town we lived in on Long Island, so we feel like national news is local news. One advantage of living in a suburb of Washington, D.C., has been the fortunate opportunity for the children to observe government up close. One disadvantage of living in a suburb of Washington, D.C., has been the unfortunate opportunity for the children to observe government up close. I felt horrified, saddened, and angered by the barrage of reports that flooded our home concerning President Clinton's scandal. I became confused and frustrated by the President's all-time high approval rating two weeks later. I felt very protective about how all of the allegations would filter through my children's ears. Frank and I were vigilant about keeping the television off and the newspapers tucked away while the kids were in the den.

Imagine my anxiety level when Jordan proclaimed one night after dinner, "Mom, I need to speak to you in private about something I heard about our President. It's very important." I took a bit longer to fill the dishwasher that evening and asked the Lord to give me wisdom. I felt angry that my little boy was forced to deal with a topic he didn't need to know about in third grade. This wasn't how we had planned for it to go. Jordan finished doing his homework, took a shower, and waited patiently for me to wipe the kitchen counters.

"Mom, are you done yet?"

I looked into his large brown eyes and reached for his thick, bear cub hands. "Let's go sit on the couch."

Jordan is a very relational, intense communicator. He turned my face toward his with both hands and seemed intensely burdened. "Mom, you have to explain something to me."

I nodded, took a deep breath, and called upon the Lord, and Jordan's eyes locked with mine. "What is it, buddy?"

Jordan looked away for a moment as if he felt a little embarrassed. He looked straight into my eyes once again and finally posed the question that he needed to have answered. "Mom . . . what's . . . an . . . intern?" I bit my bottom lip, supplied a satisfactory answer, thanked the Lord, and sent Jordan to the freezer for some bonbons.

*O*bey the government, for God is the one who put it there. All governments have been placed in power by God. . . The authorities are sent by God to help you.

—Romans 13:1, 4 (NLT)

15

Turning Forty

irthdays don't usually faze me, but I admit that reaching "halftime in the game of life" caused me to wax philosophical. A friend of mine told me a woman doesn't become interesting until she turns forty. That brought little comfort. The sobering realization was that my time on earth was half over—and *that's* if I exceed the current life-expectancy rate of women in America by two years. Of course, there's always the possibility of dying much sooner due to a mutant microbe, WWIII, or uncontrolled consumption of Italian food.

The truth is, I love my life. I love what each year has brought in terms of experiences and expansion of my heart. I love the idea that on each birthday, I'm a little wiser, a little kinder, and dare I say—a little more "conformed to His image." The Christian life is incredibly exciting for those who live it with a clear understanding of the possibilities that the Lord provides on a daily basis. I wouldn't want to be alive at any other time in history.

When I devoted my heart to Jesus as a teenager, I always felt like a second string Christian compared to the older women at the weekly Bible study who wanted Jesus to come back to earth . . . immediately. Sure, I wanted Him to return, but not right away. I secretly asked Him to wait until after I got married. Then I bargained with Him to let me experience motherhood. Now I'm asking Him to wait until the kids get married. It's not a lack of faith; it's just that I love weddings. I also love births and graduations. I love learning and feeling and holding and growing and reading and caring and giving. I have begun to understand the fragility of life and the fact that pain produces both tenderness and strength in those who love God and trust in His promises. I have even come to appreciate the dying process and its powerful effect on the living. I don't believe that's morbid—just part of loving life.

Last week, I loaded my guitar into the car and visited a retirement home in my town. Billie, a seventy-eight-year-old Prison Fellowship volunteer, and chairwoman of "The Thirty Plus Club" (of which I was made an honorary member that day), invited me to come to the center to sing for her chronies. I expected to sing a few tunes, share a few hugs, and cause some old ladies to smile. About forty women emerged from their small apartments, descended via elevator, crossed the main lobby and entered the all-purpose room. I sang to them and then we sang together ("Button Up Your Overcoat," "Sentimental Reasons," etc.). I shared a few jokes, and before I knew it, they were laughing loud and hard and thumping canes on the floor and pounding fists on their laps or walkers. Some leaned forward as their friends repeated punch lines loudly into hearing aids. It was a Kodak moment, but instead of toddlers playing in leaves or building sand castles, these were snapshots of beautiful, wise women who have lived long lives and who will soon complete their earthly sojourn.

After singing "Because He Lives," and "In His Time," I shared the Easter story and suggested that, at their age, it would behoove them to take some interest in the assurance of eternal life. They all nodded in agreement, and it was obvious that a handful had already received that blessed assurance many decades earlier. My part ended and lunch began, and three hours later, Billie walked me back to my car. I was quite taken back by the impact my "charitable" visit to the Colt's Neck Retirement Center had on *me*. Once again, I realized that I can't "outgive" God. As I drove away, I thought about the many conversations that had so deeply touched my heart.

Mildred was a phone receptionist for forty years, and her soothing, youthful, silky voice still resonated from her eighty-three-year-old, deeply wrinkled face. Harriet lost a twenty-three-year-old daughter to a brain tumor almost thirty years ago, and she could hardly contain the excitement she felt about seeing her again when they would reunite soon in heaven. Olga was born in Austria, and in her native tongue, she sang a favorite song from her childhood into my ear.

Elizabeth was an author of children's books in days long past, and she was obviously still quite proud of her articulate speech. Her hair and makeup were perfect, and she was impeccably dressed in a kelly green linen suit and fine gold jewelry. She rode around in one of those electric scooters and looked somewhat regal as she effortlessly glided across the room. Ethel was about to turn eighty and finally decided how she would celebrate. She lowered her head and stretched her neck out across the table and whispered her plan as if she didn't want anyone to steal her idea. She would request a quiet dinner at a fine restaurant with her pastor and his wife. The next morning in church, she would formally rededicate her life to the Lord. She explained that whether she had one month or several years to live, this was the most exhilarating way she could become an octogenarian.

Lilly had just turned ninety-one, and she couldn't believe that she was still alive. Nevertheless, she had plans to travel to Yosemite National Park during the summer for a huge reunion of the Franklin family. (She made sure to clarify that these were the Franklins of Philadelphia.) The extended clan meets every ten years, and the only one she ever missed was in the 1940s, because her husband and brothers were far away restoring peace to war-ravaged Europe. Martha had lost her sight except for some peripheral vision so she turned her head away to see a shadow of me. Her best friend Eleanor lives across the hall, and they have watched *Jeopardy* and *Wheel of Fortune* together for seventeen years. Eleanor was sure she would win some money if she ever became a contestant.

I'll not soon forget my visit to the "old folks home." Billie already called to invite me back next month, and I'm going to bring along a few of the blonde women (who freak out every time a new wrinkle appears). I'll also bring some candy and some Italian bread and some new jokes. I'll spend the afternoon and maybe I'll stay for dinner, and I'll listen to more stories and learn just how young and hopeful a woman can be at ninety or eighty—or even forty.

She is clothed with strength and dignity; she can laugh at the days to come.

—Proverbs 31:25 (NIV)

16

Real Men Call Home

With all respect to Professor What's-His-Name from *My Fair Lady*, his famous question is quite backwards. After all, most women have no desire to be more like men. Women are softer, kinder, and gentler then men. Women greet one another with more warmth than men do. Women send sweeter cards and longer letters. Women call and visit one another without feeling the urge to recite stats, set goals, or compete. Women help one another without seeking "win-win" scenarios. Women don't ignore their long-distance relationships just because of long-distance phone bills. Women are able to express their emotions with more ease. Women are comfortable sharing their problems, and they are very good listeners. Women are neater in the bathroom, and they know where everything goes. Women smell better than men.

When a woman leaves her house for an evening, a few days, or a week, she calls the people in that house. She lets them know where she is and how they can reach her. She checks in periodically, sometimes at the risk of hearing upsetting news about the burned dinner, the flooded laundry room, or the recent fender bender. And even though "getting away" likely means visiting her mother or sister, attending a funeral, or participating in the annual ladies' church retreat, a woman is ever mindful of the loved ones who live in her house. In the seventies we learned that real men cry. In the eighties we learned that real men eat quiche. In the nineties we learned that real men don't leave. In this new millennium I'd like to add one—real men call home. My husband (a real man), fails miserably in this fourth mandate.

When Frank started traveling for an international ministry, it was quite a major adjustment for all of us. Instead of making an occasional sales call in Chicago or Cincinnati, he was now making frequent visits to embassies and prisons in the far-flung corners of the earth. At first, I was passionate about my dissatisfaction with his phone calls, which were few and far between. With equal passion, he explained that placing a long-distance call from a prison in Zimbabwe or a church in the mountains of Peru was no easy task. Understandable.

Two years ago, Frank began taking our older children along on some of his trips. Last summer, he took our son Jordan to Africa. Jordan is my only son, and he is the only hope of carrying on the Lofaro name. Frank didn't call until the eighth day of their eighteen-day trip. *Not* understandable. We exchanged Italian emotions on the phone that day, and Frank was sure to have Jordan call home every third day thereafter. Two weeks of work in the field culminated in three days of safari. Imagine my thoughts when Jordan called one morning to tell me that a year earlier, a woman had been attacked by a lion outside of the very lodge where they were staying. My last words to Jordan that day were, "Never get out of the Jeep, sit close to the man with the rifle, and put Daddy on the phone RIGHT NOW!" I expressed some more Italian emotions.

Our oldest child Paris has had the privilege of visiting three continents with her Dad. While I don't subscribe to the parent-child relational theories of Sigmund Freud, I will assert that Frank and Paris are alike in many ways and have a very special closeness. In an effort to maintain and enhance that close bond, Frank did some research and found a father-daughter high adventure camp. The camp offers father-son as well as father-daughter week-long programs in order for dads to enter into deeper relationships with their twelve- to eighteen-year-old children. The day starts with devotions, a hearty breakfast, one-on-one discussion time about key issues, and after lunch, the afternoon is spent participating in outdoor challenges that often result in getting drenched, scraped, and sore. After dinner, each day ends with a service that includes worship and a message given by a special speaker. The brochure sounded terrific, and this was one trip that caused me little worry.

They attended the J. H. Ranch just south of the Oregon border during the first week of August. Frank warned ahead of time that there was only one pay phone on the property and that I should not expect a lot of calls. One finally came the fourth day after they arrived.

"Hey El, it's me."

"Honey! We've missed you two! Couldn't you call any sooner? Is everything okay? How was the flight? How is the camp? How is the food? How is my precious Paris?"

"Everything is fine. They've put together an impressive program. You wouldn't believe the white-water rafting trip we took yesterday or the rock climbing the day before. Tomorrow we're taking a ropes course over forty feet in the air. They do a great job tying the daytime physical challenges into the talks at night. The speakers are powerful, and they're covering all the topics you'd ever want a kid to hear. Wow, talk about *positive* peer pressure! The weather has been good, a little chilly at night. And, oh yeah—Paris got her period."

The conversation halted for a fairly long pause. I felt my mouth open slowly and my forehead scrunch. I held my own private moment of silence. *Paris got her period? How could that happen while she is so far away from me? I have waited twelve years for this! We've had chats. We've discussed products. We were going to cry and giggle and hug and go out for lunch when it finally happened. We never even got to the topic of Motrin.* I took a deep breath, pursed my lips, and unscrunched my forehead as much as possible.

"Ellie, are you still there? Hello?"

"Yeah, I'm here. Paris got WHAT? When did THAT happen?"

"On the day we got here."

"That was four days ago! How could you not call me about this? Are you crazy? Don't you remember anything you heard about communication on our last marriage retreat? Answer me!"

"Cut it out, honey. She's fine. Do you want to talk to her?"

"Yes! Of course! Put my baby on!"

"Hi, Mom. This place is great! You wouldn't believe all they have planned for us."

I felt my face get very hot and found myself holding back tears. "Paris, are you okay? Do you want to come home? Do you have cramps? Were you scared? Did you feel alone? Is Daddy helping you? Does he know what's going on?"

"Mom, I'm fine. Daddy took me to a drugstore. Everything is great. Love you—gotta go. We're discussing guys, dating, and sex today. Tell the kids I miss them. Bye!" Click.

To say I felt left out would be a gross understatement. My husband wanted to bond with our exceptional preadolescent and he did. He wanted to set ground rules for her teenage years and he did. He wanted her to understand what role he would have as the man in her life and he did. He wanted to create an agreeable framework for conflict resolution. He wanted to set worthy goals that she could achieve. He wanted her to hear the stark statistics and to clearly illustrate "win-win" scenarios she will enjoy if she plays by the rules. On the last night of camp, the girls professed vows of purity to their earthly fathers and to their Heavenly One. Frank presented her with a special ring, which will be replaced at an altar, if the Lord wills. He handed her letters from special people in her life affirming her value and her destiny in Christ. He wanted to make her understand that love is very often misunderstood. He wanted Paris Lofaro to know she was the most cherished twelve-year-old on the planet—and he did.

I suppose there are times when it's all right for men to act like men. But I still say we smell better.

You fathers—if your children ask for a fish, do you give them a snake instead? Or if they ask for an egg, do you give them a scorpion? Of course not! If you sinful people know how to give good gifts to your children, how much more will your heavenly Father give the Holy Spirit to those who ask him."
—Luke 11:11-13 (NLT)

17

Easter in Prison

I spent an Easter weekend in prison. Not a lily, new hat, or pair of patent-leather shoes in sight. No chocolate, no marshmallow chicks, no ham and turkey dinners. Nothing felt familiar about this particular Easter weekend. Endless country roads, bunker housing, large gates, a guard tower, the dogs, barbed wire with large razor blades—these ominous signs seemed strangely fitting for a gray and drizzly Good Friday. Although the prisoner named Jesus was an innocent man, my urge to be metaphorical was strong. I have based my entire existence on the fact that Jesus rose from the dead and that all who believe will do the same. Perhaps some prisoners would be encouraged to hear His story. The prospect of speaking with the inmates face-to-face felt somewhat intimidating. I took a long, deep breath before walking through the visitors' gate.

Prison Fellowship (the ministry that forced me to leave my happy life on Long Island so I could be a supportive wife when Frank heard God's call) has created a powerful initiative called The Starting Line. In short, it's an all-out evangelical blitz of the prison population within a particular state. The eighteen-month preparation period and detailed logistics are mind-boggling. When all of the official, administrative, and financial details are set, a team arrives for several days. The team consists of musicians, athletes, comedians, and inspirational speakers. They hold a rally in a different prison each day for almost a week, and then another team arrives and continues until every prison in the area has been visited. The inmates are entertained and edified. Hundreds of Bibles are distributed. Locally trained volunteers attend the rally nearest their homes and then commit to doing follow-up. The Starting Line has helped prisoners enter into the most important race of their lives.

The programs I attended took place in South Carolina. Our ministry team visited women's prisons in and around Columbia. Frank and the kids drove me to the airport and, as I kissed them all good-bye, I was mindful about the vastly different world I would soon be entering voluntarily and exiting gladly. I said my good-byes.

"I love you soooooo much! Don't forget to pray for me. Mommy is going to tell some ladies about Jesus. Save me some Easter goodies. I'll see you in a few days."

They drove off and I teared up. Italians don't even eat out Easter weekend, let alone visit prisoners. The relatives just didn't understand.

"Prisoners? You care about prisoners? Take care of your own family and forget those louses! They should rot in hell for the things they've done! This God stuff is really getting carried away!" And that was my sweet aunt talking! I'll leave the unsolicited commentary by my loved ones from Brooklyn up to your imagination.

I met up with the PF group at the Columbia Holiday Inn, and we set off on a two-hour trek to the Leath Women's Correctional Facility. As I let out a long, deep breath at the visitors' gate, I passed through the metal detector and then was asked to remove my shoes. After a thorough body search, we were escorted into a holding room with thick steel sliding doors on two sides. I realized at that point that we were "locked in."

We proceeded down to a small gym with one section of bleachers. I learned earlier in the day that Leath was a medium-security facility with 350 women. About 200 of them opted to attend The Starting Line program that night, and as they streamed in from their quads, I was completely astounded by what seemed like a cruel surprise. They were young. They were so young. They were well groomed and neatly dressed. They were pretty. Lord, how can this be? It looks like a high school pep rally. What have they done? Why are they here? Where are their parents? Save them, Jesus. The program was powerful, the salvation message tearful, the brief conversations unforgettable, the Lord ever faithful. Many came to salvation that night and learned of a freedom they had never known.

The next day, our itinerary brought us to the Broad River Facility, the largest maximum-security prison in South Carolina. It was actually a campus of several prisons on the same property. About half of the three hundred female inmates attended the program on Easter eve. The hardness in some of the women was countered by the undeniable glow in others who rushed to the front seats, Bibles in hand. They were the same ones who knew every word the guest artist sang to them and completed every verse the speaker quoted. Some of these precious sisters brought fellow inmates along hoping to introduce them to the One who had provided hope and meaning to their fractured lives.

Through the power of prayer and the grace of the Savior, many responded to the salvation message—suddenly transformed from bondage to freedom, darkness to light, pain to comfort, fear to peace. Some cried loudly from a hollow place I had never heard before. Some wept quietly. Some held friends tightly in a huddle and some dropped to their knees. I prayed with several women and turned to see my friend walking toward me with her arm around the shoulder of a young, sweet-looking inmate who had come forward. My friend's eye contact was intense. "Ellie, this is Susan Smith. I told her you have young children and . . ." Her voice trailed off as she was interrupted and pulled in another direction. So there I stood, looking into the eyes of the infamous young mother who no longer had young children. The longest ten seconds of my life passed as I groped for words.

The conversation I had with Susan Smith that night told me more about myself than about her. I wrestled during that fifteen-minute encounter and in the weeks that followed. Did I really believe Jesus died for every sinner? *Did I assign different judgments to different sins? Would the thief on the cross be in paradise if he were the rapist on the cross? How about the child molester on the cross? Did Saul of Tarsus kill innocent people?*

Were some tortured? Does God love Susan Smith and her children as much as He loves me and mine? Is salvation really free?

I knew the correct answers in my heart, but my head did not want to cooperate. The guards began to clear the room, so I finished praying and hugged Susan good-bye. As tears rolled down her cheeks, I couldn't help but remember the night her heinous act was exposed on network news. I had a fleeting thought of which I am ashamed. I decided that Susan Smith should suffer a slow death. It was clear through our conversation that she is, indeed, dying every day. May God have mercy on *me*.

Salvation reverses everything and brings about the unexpected—including resurrection. Christ's work on the cross overrules our reason, pushes us outside our comfort zones, and deflates our self-righteousness.

That proved to be the best Easter I've ever had. How will I explain that to my relatives?

For it is by grace you have been saved, through faith—and this not from yourselves, it is the gift of God—not by works, so that no one can boast. For we are God's workmanship, created in Christ Jesus to do good works, which God prepared in advance for us to do.

—Ephesians 2:8-10 (NIV)

18

Life Is Beautiful

I am sure that many of you have seen the film *Life Is Beautiful*. When it was first released in October 1998, it was shown in only a limited market, but with unprecedented accolades and seven American Academy Award nominations, the film received astounding attention. The film has an uncanny power to convinc ingly deliver the message that life is beautiful, even in and through life's greatest tragedies. For me, seeing the film was a defining moment. The two most striking aspects of this experience are (1) that I saw it with my Italian mother (the film is in Italian with English subtitles) and (2) the central theme of sacrificial love unto death—more specifically, the love of a father for his son.

Allow me to expound upon the Italian component. The first half of the movie is pure romantic comedy, set in northern Italy in the 1940s. Roberto Begnini (director, scriptwriter, and lead actor) masterfully portrays a clownish man who pursues his beautiful "Principessa" and wins her with his wit, perseverance, and love. Imagine how my enjoyment of this delightful segment was enhanced by my mother's outbursts of hilarious laughter. I cannot recall ever hearing her laugh like she did that day. Begnini's script doubled her over in sidesplitting heaves, but I couldn't even turn my eyes in her direction for fear of missing the subtitles. Begnini's character, Guido, wins the woman of his dreams (and his real-life wife), Dora, and together they have a son, Joshua.

As quickly as one can turn a page, the tone and setting of the film grow somber. Guido and Joshua are arrested for being Jewish and are herded onto a long line of cattle cars heading for a death camp in Germany. Dora races to the depot and insists that she too be allowed on the train. The Nazi officer tells her to mind her own business and go home. But Dora insists on sharing the fate that awaits her husband and son, and although she is not of Jewish ancestry, she demands a place on the train. The Nazi smirks, and Dora boards a car full of Jewish women and girls. What follows in the next hour is some of the most tear-jerking, heartwarming, gut-wrenching, life-affirming cinema that I have ever seen. Pain and joy? Warmth and terror? How can these emotions mingle? How can a movie about the Holocaust be called *Life Is Beautiful?*

Jesus said that "Greater love hath no man than this, that a man lay down his life for his friends" (John 15:13, KJV). That is a very beautiful, yet nearly impossible concept for most of us to grasp, and the film shows that love in action. I could not stop thinking about that level of sacrificial love for days after seeing the film.

The phone rang late one evening. As usual, Mom was checking to make sure we made it home safely, and to ask how the kids were, and to tell me that the movie had caused her to remember something that had been suppressed into the recesses of her memory bank since 1945. What she told me was quite remarkable, and she gave me permission to repeat it.

My mother entered the world as Alessandra Bermani. She was born in northern Italy in 1934 and moved with her parents to Tripoli in northern Africa during her early childhood. Mussolini had taken this region, and my grandfather was "armbanded" and "strongly encouraged" by the Fascists to assist in the industrialization of Tripoli. In 1945 just before the end of WWII, my mother was eleven years old. The social and political unrest boiled, and Jewish persecution continued in full, ugly force. Angry factions dragged Jews up to the balconies of apartment buildings and threw them over the railings into the streets.

One late afternoon, Alessandra was left alone in her apartment for a short while. My grandmother ran out to the market with the babies, and my grandfather had not yet returned from the machine factory. Glancing out a window and down into the street, my mother made eye contact with a woman who was being chased by a violent mob of men.

Within seconds, the woman began pounding on the door, begging entrance. Without hesitation, my mother let her in and slammed the door shut within inches of the mob's deafening arrival. The Jewish woman collapsed to the floor and crawled down the long hallway and under my grandparents' bed. The eleven-year-old Alessandra bolted the three locks, put her small shoulder under the doorknob, and leaned her little body against the solid wood, ten-foot door for the most terrifying ten minutes of her life.

She heard the threats. She heard the bargaining. She watched the thick metal hinges loosen. She felt her knees weaken as the door begin to buckle. She cried out to God. My mother never found out why the band of attackers suddenly dispersed that day. The sobbing woman crawled out from under the bed and stooped down, attempting to kiss my mother's feet. She finally stood, hugged my mother, and fled when she saw that the street was clear. My mother returned the embrace, and filled with fear, shock, and relief, she bolted the locks once again. Then something happened that was so painful that she chose not to remember it until almost fifty-five years later. Seeing *Life Is Beautiful* triggered the memory that had been buried deep within her.

She began to bleed. She bled from her nose. The blood did not trickle, it gushed. The bleeding was profuse, and when she finally stopped the flow, she began to bleed vaginally, which horrified the eleven-year-old who had not yet experienced her menstrual cycle. Blood surged from her body, and then Nana returned from the market, shocked at the sight before her and terrified by her child's tale of what had taken place during her brief absence. She chastised Alessandra for opening the door and held her closely.

Before we hung up the phone, Mom told me that her childhood ended that day. I was speechless. *My mother saved a Jewish life during the Holocaust.* What an incredible revelation. I have no idea what price she paid to do that. She certainly did not pause to assess the cost.

I would like to think that I would risk my life for another human being, just like my mother did. And I would like to believe that I would have gotten on that train with my husband and child, just like Dora did. And I would definitely do everything in my power to shield my child from the horrors of a concentration camp, just like Guido did. But I cannot fathom *allowing*—no, *arranging*—for my child to die in someone else's place, just like God did. I cannot comprehend how and why He would give up His only son. I cannot grasp why He sacrificed His precious baby. Why would a father send his son to experience pain, ridicule, and death? I will never understand how a child could be born for the sole purpose of dying. *Why God? Why You? Why Him? Why on a cross? Oh God, may I begin to understand that level of love. I need a new heart . . . renew my mind, Lord.*

Jesus said He came into the world to give life; life more abundantly. When I was younger in my faith, I wanted to believe the "abundantly" meant only obvious blessings. I have since come to realize that the Lord uses all of life; the good and evil, the plenty and want, the beautiful and ugly—in order to conform us to His image. Jesus hung on a cross because of His perfect love. Sheila Walsh calls Good Friday "a scandalous, glorious night." God used the worst circumstance a person could endure to bring about the most wonderful possibilities for mankind to enjoy. He allowed His Son to suffer an ugly death so that all who believe in Him could know a beautiful life—now and forever.

Can you say life is beautiful? I don't mean one without heartache and sorrow. Jesus was well acquainted with those companions. He once asked His disciples, "Who do you say I am?" Everything rides on your answer to that question.

This is how God showed his love among us: He sent his one and only Son into the world that we might live through him. This is love: not that we loved God, but that he loved us and sent his Son as an atoning sacrifice for our sins.

—1 John 4:9-10 (NIV)

19

A Tribute

The institution known as "the family" has been under attack
since its inception. (Begin in Genesis 3 and read on.) Satan
hates strong families. His daily goal is to break us down, to
divide us, to cause strife, guilt, envy, unrest, shame, hatred, anger, and
rejection—shall I continue? In this modern age of microwaves, cell
phones, and the ready claim of "I'm a victim," finger pointing and
parent bashing have become the norm. Dennis Rainey (a well-
respected author and the Director of Family Life, a ministry of
Campus Crusade for Christ), has written a book entitled *The Tribute*
in which he presents a convincing thesis about the responsibility
and the joy of fulfilling the fifth commandment in a practical, tangible way. Presenting a tribute to our parents is a powerful testament
to what God can accomplish if we humble ourselves and express
our thankfulness.

If you are like me, you did not grow up with Ozzie and
Harriet. You may even be tempted to say that your home was "dysfunctional"; take a number! Rainey deals with a wide array of scenarios in which people have joyfully given tributes to their wonderful (and not so wonderful) mothers and fathers. I highly recommend this book and exhort you not to wait for sickness and death
to share your unspoken love and thanks with those you hold dear.
After we read Rainey's book, my sweet husband presented a tribute

to his mom. He had it professionally printed and framed and included a photo of the two of them at the bottom. Guess what was hanging inside Pearl Lofaro's front door the very next day? And so, with a humble and thankful heart, I pay public tribute to my father, Albert Mannarino. He celebrated his seventieth birthday on March 3, 1999.

Dear Dad,

I have so many wonderful memories of you. When we moved from Brooklyn to East Northport, you took on a bigger mortgage and a much bigger yard. I remember standing behind you on the riding mower and squeezing your neck tightly so I wouldn't get sucked underneath. You enthusiastically took all five kids to your softball games in Huntington and bought us ice cream from the Bungalow Bar Man between innings. I watched intently as you struck your opponents out with your lightening fast windmill pitches. When I was nine, you bought me my first baseball glove—it was a Mel Stottlemeyer Special, and I pitched a no-hit game with it in high school. I still have it.

When I went from being a Brownie to a Girl Scout, you took the cookie order form to work for a whole week, and I sold the most cookies of any girl in any troop that year. I have warm memories of going to visit you at work. At the time, you were stationed at the Sears in Hicksville. When Mom got all five of us out of the car, she could barely hold us back as we ran through the doors, around the corner past the vacuums, and then past the sewing machines toward the Allstate Insurance booth. The most handsome man in the world could be found there, and we always flew into your outstretched arms. I can still recall the reassuring scent of your Old Spice aftershave.

I have always admired the love you held in your heart for your own mother and father. You were a good son. I remember the weekly drives to Brooklyn and my acute bouts of car sickness, which temporarily subsided when we entered the tunnel and you allowed us to lower the windows, stick out our heads, and scream at the top of our lungs. The weekly pilgrimage to Brooklyn was also memorable for the frenzied tribal chant that you so passionately conducted: "Hidey, Heedy, Hadey, Ho." I remember how you cried when your "Mama" passed away and how you cried even harder the first time we visited her in the mausoleum. I was strangely warmed as I gazed at the name Elvira Mannarino—my own—which was inscribed into the marble. I know a part of you died with her.

When you were forty (at the time, I thought that was old!), your eldest was twelve and your baby was five, and you took two major risks. You left an established national insurance giant to venture out on your own, and you brought your family to a wonderful place called Dix Hills. I can still see you building that blue stone wall and shoveling dirt into grates until sundown in order to remove all the rocks and pebbles before the sod was laid. You were the "mayor" of the neighborhood, and your barbecues and pool parties were always the best. You even allowed forty-seven college kids to sleep over and made a hot breakfast for each one. You did all the work and allowed me to shine. We had so many great times in that back yard.

You gave me an appreciation for good food and fine restaurants. I marveled as you walked into pork stores, delis, and bakeries each and every weekend to order the freshest, most delectable offerings of the day. Saturdays were always a treat at the Mannarino household. I thought every kid had deli and fresh malted milkshakes for lunch. I always appreciated your devotion to family life. You were home at 5:15, and Mom had dinner on the table at 5:30 sharp every weeknight. You cared about our manners and our homework, and you came to our games whenever you could.

I have always admired your work ethic. Because

of your extreme generosity, I never worried that I wouldn't have the things I needed or wanted. You were always a wonderful provider, and I do not have any memory of your complaining about your heavy load. You helped support me through college and provided a car so I could student teach in the suburbs of Boston. During the summers, I worked part time for the Mannarino Insurance Agency, and you were patient with me even when I opened all four drawers of the tall filing cabinet at the same time!

Although your own dream to study art at UCLA was cut short due to finances, you dutifully returned home to work odd jobs and attend college at night. You studied insurance and went on to become a top producer. When we were little, we sometimes accompanied you on summer nights when you visited people's homes to discuss their policies. Invariably, the lady of the house would learn you had a few kids in the car, and we would be waved in for cake or cookies.

God desires for me to honor you—and I do. The hard times as well as the good times have taught me so much. I have learned a great deal from you. I am very thankful you are my dad and that you are Grandpa to my children. Words seem so inadequate to express all that I feel. Thank you for everything you have done for me, but most of all, thank you for your love. I have never doubted that you were proud to be my father—and that has contributed greatly to the woman I have become today.

I love you, Daddy.

Ellie

*H*onor your father and mother, that you may have a long, good life in the land the Lord your God will give you.

—Exodus 20:12 (TLB)

20

Don't Look Back

iding a mountain bike down the slope of a dormant volcano is quite a popular activity on the island of Maui. Frank and I enjoyed that experience in the late eighties when we were there for a trade show. Ten years later, we returned to the island paradise with our two mothers and three children. It was a sweet reunion, since we don't see our moms often enough. Frank had been traveling extensively throughout Asia to complete a number of projects for Prison Fellowship International. My husband has many gifts, not the least of which is his ability to be a terrific vacation coordinator. He took care of every detail, including the rental of snorkeling equipment for the kids. How wonderful.

He was very pleased with himself for arranging a bike excursion down the Haleakala volcano for our mothers, our oldest daughter, and me. Our mothers simultaneously objected when Frank proudly announced these plans the night before the "outing" was to take place. Pearl Lofaro had not ridden a bike in thirty years, and Alessandra Mannarino hadn't touched one in twenty. Frank assured them that it is impossible to forget how to ride a bicycle, that there was no danger involved. He explained that riders only had to use finger muscles to occasionally brake as they coasted down the thirty-five-mile, gently curving road. Frank addressed all of their concerns, informed them that he had prepaid the bike company, and promised that it would be a fabulous female bonding experience. He wondered how they could deprive our daughter Paris of this once in a lifetime memory with her grandmothers. How persuasive.

I am not a morning person by nature (new nature or old), so when the 4 am courtesy wake-up call came through, I didn't exactly start the day with a song in my heart—although I do recall murmuring something about my need for female bonding being way down on my list in relation to my need for sleep. How ungrateful.

The four of us met in the lobby, and a large van promptly pulled up at 5 am The driver, "Dan the Man," jumped out, checked off our names, and cheerfully welcomed us. We were to drive one hour toward the volcano, hitch on a trailer full of bikes and gear, and pick up another van driver so Dan could be our line leader on a bike. Next we planned to drive another hour up the volcano as the sun rose. Then we would "suit up," climb on the mountain bikes, stop for a prearranged picnic lunch halfway down the volcano, and finish the ride in a quaint little town on the west side of the island. How lovely.

We picked up passengers at other hotels and introductions and niceties were exchanged. To my surprise (and initial disbelief) each passenger expressed devotion to God and sincere pursuit of the Christian life. What a delight. Well, the delight was short-lived. It ended when the Doctrinal Differences Docudrama began—quite a doozy, and Dan the Man got very quiet. The couple from Chuck Smith's church were experts on the end times. They had the latest information concerning the roles Turkey and Iran will play, and the husband gave a blow-by-blow account of what we can expect to see in the coming months. He included some gruesome description of chemical warfare and how it will be used by enemies of Israel but will backfire because of "natural" disasters.

The young bride from Chattanooga warned the couple from California not to ever take Scripture out of context nor to speculate about God's mysterious ways. She attended the same church as Kay Arthur. The guy who worshiped at Kenneth Copeland's church didn't think anything needed to be mysterious about a living, vibrant God and challenged the young bride to take the Lord at His word for all things. He went on to explain that her new husband didn't have to be back in the hotel room feeling sick if he really understood God's promises. The conversation somehow shifted to Mother Teresa, and when the fellow from Calvary Chapel suggested the good Mother wasn't saved, my own good mother proceeded to eat him for an early lunch. I kept my opinions to myself (for a change) and took lots of mental notes.

Real life is so much more interesting than the movies! My good mother-in-law gave a "love one another" speech, and we spent the last leg of the ascent talking about the scenery and the weather. Dan the Man seemed relieved not to be a Christian. How regrettable.

We finally arrived at the peak of Haleakala (House of the Sun), and the view was breathtaking. We were ten thousand feet above sea level, the sun was rising, the air was quite chilly, and we all piled out to receive final instructions from our fearless leader, Dan. When his assistant unlocked the doors of the trailer, we saw a rack of mountain bikes, a rack of heavy-duty helmets, and large boxes filled with jackets, pants, and gloves. Those of us wearing shorts felt encouraged.

My mother was the first to "suit up," and while she did so, my mother-in-law mounted a bike and went for a test drive. She easily rode fifty yards across the parking lot and we cheered her on and then she suddenly did a Charlie Chaplin impersonation. She stopped pedaling, the bike came to a dead halt, and she and the bike began to fall over in slow motion. Frank's mom remained glued to the handlebars, the seat, and pedals. Ouch! Dan and I immediately ran to help her up. Thank the Lord, she was okay. As she uttered, "I told you so," I looked back toward the van to find my mother removing her rubber pants. (Her jacket, gloves, and helmet had already been returned to the driver.) We soon started our descent, and the grandmas gladly rode behind us in the van. How satisfying.

Since Paris was the youngest rider, Dan decided she would be at the head of the line, just behind him. I followed behind my precious firstborn child (maternal instincts), and the rest of the sanctified souls lined up behind me and in front of the newly named "Gram-Van." We soon picked up speeds of twenty miles per hour, and I was so grateful for the protective gear. Our fingers would have surely frozen were it not for the thick nylon gloves.

Paris was exuberant and started swaying her shoulders, shouting joyous exclamations and singing "Born to Be Wild." As we approached a sharp switchback, I suspected that this kid was not paying close attention to the road. I came alongside of her (like the fine protector that I am) and offered some wise counsel and a couple of threats. To my relief, she sat straight and grew quiet for the next mile. I observed that the black volcanic rocks, which blanketed the roadside, seemed awfully jagged and ominous. Some were more than a foot in diameter. The road seemed steeper and narrower than I had remembered. A man-made, five-inch, square curb had been added between the pavement and the large rocks. I wondered what changed more in the decade that had passed, the mountain or me? The view at forty was quite different than the one I enjoyed at thirty. How revealing.

We were only about ten minutes into the downhill experience when I did what Dan instructed us not to do ... I looked back. I had to. I wanted to be sure the lonely bride from Chattanooga wasn't too close on my tail. I wanted to see what the line looked like. I felt responsible to check if the Gram-Van was still with us. Rather than being turned into a pillar of salt (although, that might have been preferable), I turned around in time to watch my front tire hit that ridiculous man-made curb that wasn't there ten years earlier. The rest is history. The bike is history. The emergency room is history. As my body morphed with the volcanic rocks, I thought I was history. I'm not being dramatic. Imagine what I felt as I laid there on my back in a full spread eagle.

I felt intense pain. I broke the fall with my right hand, smashing the wrist and forearm. My right shin and thigh were on fire. My ribs felt broken at the point of handlebar "insertion."

I felt embarrassed. I had just explained to the mothers how ridiculous their fears were and how safe the ride was. I had told the Kenneth Copeland guy how athletic I was. I had warned Paris to pay attention. I had broken a rule. I had wondered what the van driver behind us said on the radio to alert Dan, who was still moving ahead of me. Perhaps, "Disobedient woman down!" or maybe, "Smug New Yorker taken out!" How embarrassing.

I felt afraid. Dan looked down and asked if I needed an ambulance. How would I know? Did I *look* like I needed an ambulance? My mother knelt beside me, and as the group gathered around in a circle, she began to weep. In her lovely Italian accent Mom wailed, "She is too nice for this! Why did it have to be Ellie?" Too nice for what? Did I look worse than I felt? Was a limb hanging? Was blood oozing? As Mom continued to make nonprofessional medical commentary, my mother-in-law ordered her back to the van. I found my breath and then my voice, asked if my leg was bleeding, declined the ambulance, and cradled my right wrist. How depressing.

My next request brought immediate response. A flurry of hands touched my hurting body, and prayers were both loudly and silently lifted toward heaven. Denominational discord vanished, replaced by the unity that comes with difficulty. Dan and his assistant absorbed it all. My helmet was lifted off and I walked to the van with a throbbing wrist, a serious limp, and a bruised ego. Since I was not bleeding and my broken bone could wait two hours, I opted to finish the trip in the van. I did not wish to disrupt the day any further, nor did I wish to upset Paris, who was having a grand time.

Dan later drove me to the emergency room of Maui Central, and I had the opportunity to lovingly communicate the gospel. He promised me he would look into it, and I promised him I wouldn't look back. Just before the X rays were taken of my right arm and leg, the doctor advised me that the wrist was obviously broken. I thanked him for the thorough exam and advised him not to be too sure. I explained the mountaintop prayer vigil. He smirked at the nurse. Christmas music played over the PA system.

I waited for a long time in the examination room. In disbelief, the doctor returned to report that I had no broken bones. I let out a joyous, audible praise, and he conceded I was getting an early Christmas present. After wrapping my sprained arm in a one-week cast, he smiled and said good-bye. As he exited the room, he turned to the nurse and murmured, "Two points for prayer." How divine.

*Heal me, O Lord, and I shall be healed; Save me,
and I shall be saved, For You are my praise.*
—Jeremiah 17:14 (NKJV)

21

Things that Rust

In 1985 B.C. (before children), Frank and I bought a brand-new Honda Accord. It was functional, fuel efficient, and dependable. It was a comfortable, contemporary, attractive silver car. Over the years, it has certainly had its share of dinks and dents, of scrapes and scratches, of wheel-well rot and rust. I had hoped that Frank would sell it before we made the move from New York to Virginia in 1994. After all, we got excellent use of the vehicle for ten years and certainly could not be accused of squandering money on cars. The only car we ever purchased after the '85 Honda Accord was a '91 Volvo wagon. The Volvo salesman guaranteed that the kids would be safe in it and boasted about what attractive lines it had. Never mind the fact that it looked like a hearse and had charcoal gray interior and exterior—real mood lifters. The days of form gave way to function as we adjusted our tastes and started buying products touted at the top of consumer safety lists. If you really loved your baby in the eighties, then you were forced to buy the Century car seat, the Graco porta-crib, the Fisher Price highchair, and the wildly popular Aprica stroller from Italy.

I left all our baby gear (junk) in New York when we moved. I was happy (eager) to share (unload) all of it onto friends and relatives who would put it to good use. As a matter of fact, I left lots of stuff in New York. I felt an out-of-state move would force me to do the ultimate spring-cleaning. It was truly a purging experience:

new state, new house, new friends, new job, new church, new school. Surely, we would want to sell the ten-year-old, very used Honda and buy a new car. Frank didn't agree.

He insisted that the car was in very good condition. I told him it had become a deathtrap. He insisted that it would serve him well, since we bought a home just three miles from work. I told him he could buy a red moped. He insisted that it was still quite functional, fuel efficient, and dependable. I told him it was an eyesore. He insisted that we needed to be extra prudent about any specious buying now that we were in the ministry.

And so, since 1994, Frank J. Lofaro, Jr. has driven a rusty old Honda to the offices of Prison Fellowship. He actually loves the car and boasts to everyone who will listen that it has 157,000 miles on it. One of his favorite expressions is, "Ya can't kill a Honda!" I've decided it makes him feel more humble in some sort of prideful way. He adamantly denies this accusation.

Naturally, the Honda has experienced more wear and tear since our move. The left front tire wobbles. The rust spots have expanded. The radio only gets AM reception, and the lid on the gas tank always jams. I have declared it off-limits for the children. Recently, when we drove the Honda to pick up some African guests at Dulles International Airport because the Volvo was being serviced, our friends told Frank he was "mocking the poor" with his car. They let him know they owned much nicer vehicles back in Zimbabwe. Finally, I had found some allies. When the Volvo broke down and needed towing twice in one week, I had finally gained my husband's attention about the need to assess our family's automotive needs.

After days of painful deliberation, Frank decided to part with his Honda. We spent two thousand dollars on the Volvo, placed the Accord in the local paper, and went shopping for something brand-new for me to drive during the week and for family use on weekends. Naturally, I wanted what every good mother wants for her darling children—a minivan. I read. I studied. I researched. I went on the Internet. I was well prepared for the hunt. A minivan would be a perfect choice since safety was my first priority. Frank didn't agree.

After four cross-examinations, I concluded that the thought of driving a minivan was a threat to Frank's masculinity. He tried to explain to me that owning a minivan would be the ultimate surrender to all that is predictable, passive, and bland about suburbia. He asked me to have compassion and to see things through his eyes. So, being the kind, submissive wife that I am, I advised him to get counseling. He refused and pressed the case for the ever-popular SUV. I am not particularly fond of those things. They're big. They're loud. They guzzle gas. They're hard to park. You climb up into them and fall down out of them. I test drove the Expedition and the Navigator. I had the ingenious idea of test driving the Navigator straight to my house. It didn't fit in the garage. Thank you, Lord!

What is this craze with SUVs? How gigantic does a vehicle have to be in order for people to feel safe? Just when I think I've seen the biggest one, they roll an even bigger one off the assembly line. Ford, Chevy, Toyota, and even Lincoln and Cadillac have joined the act. Have you been inside one? You feel as though you have just entered a ride at Six Flags. I'm suggesting they be called ETVs (End Times Vehicles). Fearful of food shortages? Own an ETV and all of your worries will be over. They can seat the entire soccer team, hold a year's supply of food, and haul your house on a special trailer hitch. Want to avoid the mark of the beast? With an ETV, you can use the built-in compass to drive over the river, through the woods, and up the mountain to escape. I became convinced we had to own one. Frank agreed.

Six dealerships, four test drives, and two Saturday afternoons later, we were the owners of a new Dodge Durango. It's a "manageable" SUV that can seat a family of five plus two grandmothers, and it fits into the garage. When we arrived home that day, there were nine callers responding to the ad for the rusty car. Most were men, some had foreign accents, and all had hopes of owning an '85 Honda. We ended up selling the car to a young man named Pedro from El Salvador. He explained, in broken English, that he and his wife had asked God to bless them with a better car in time for the arrival of their first baby. I whispered to Frank to lower the price, but God had apparently beaten me to it. We encouraged Pedro to use the savings to buy something for the new baby, maybe the best car seat on the market. The proud, soon-to-be papa beamed and drove away, quite pleased and grateful for the Lord's provisions.

I couldn't help thinking about the neighbor with the new Mercedes who just left his wife and children. There is no question in my mind about which of the two men has more wealth and joy. Pedro got a new car. His baby got a new car seat. And I got a new revelation about wants and needs—giving and getting—having and sharing. We should all consider the many blessings in our lives and the enormous surplus that we too often take for granted. We must guard our hearts against the monsters of materialism and the demons of dissatisfaction. Count yourself wealthy because you know God. Count yourself joyful because you love God. Count yourself blessed because He loves you. What great news that is.

> Do not store up for yourselves treasures on earth, where moth and rust destroy, and where thieves break in and steal. But store up for yourselves treasures in heaven, where moth and rust do not destroy, and where thieves do not break in and steal. For where your treasure is, there your heart will be also.
>
> —Matthew 6:19-21 (NIV)

22

Of Golf and God

I don't understand the whole love affair with the game of golf. Personally, I have a strong aversion to it. I'd say I hate it, but that doesn't sound very Christian. I don't like playing it. I don't like watching it. I don't like listening to people talk about it. I don't even like going into golf stores. Everything they sell is ridiculously expensive. The game is costly in terms of both time and money, and its effect on family life can be devastating.

Recent statistics released by NAAAG (National Association of Adults Against Golf) show that the number of golf widows is on the rise. There are adorable little golf orphans in nice homes throughout the country. Many a family outing has been canceled at the last minute due to the unexplainable fever that comes over golfers during the back nine. This group wears golf shirts, golf shoes, and golf socks. They drink from golf mugs, read books on golf wisdom, tell golf lore, and speak fluent golfese. You haven't been fully bored to tears until you've listened to devotees discuss every detailed description of their putts, pars, bogeys, birdies, duffs, divots, strokes, swings, links, greens, holes, traps, drives, and chips. Do the rest of us really need to have this information? Give me long-winded fishermen any day! At least their stories have colors besides green!

One of our neighbors had invited six couples to a barbecue on a late Sunday afternoon. I was excited at the thought of getting to know some neighbors and enjoying the fine art of conversation.

Imagine my disappointment when the host husband invited the guest husbands to his basement home theater to watch "the end" (they were down there an hour) of a major golf championship on his digital, wide-screen, surround-sound television. I understand surround sound for Jurassic Park—but for golf? Were they going to be blown away by the sound of the ball dropping into the cup? Or maybe they would get chills hearing the swing of the club in full-blown stereo. Whatever. I chose to enjoy the little women who were left behind to discuss summer recreational options for their offspring.

As the hostess began to clear away the dishes and wrap the leftovers, a loud eruption of shouts, hoops, and hollers emanated from down below. We all filed down to examine the elation. We entered the rec room to find seven grown men shrieking, high-fiving, jumping about, raising clenched fists in the air and looking very much like they had just been visited by Ed McMahon. What a sight. All the hoopla was over some guy who sank a twenty-foot putt. The exuberance quelled, and we all stepped outside onto the deck to enjoy desserts and the conclusion of what turned out to be a lovely evening.

Conversation turned to "religiosity," and Frank fielded some typical questions. Yes, Chuck Colson really had a genuine conversion since Watergate. No, there are no prisoners housed in the office complex of Prison Fellowship. Yes, we're Christian. No, not any particular denomination. Yes, our pastor is an African American. No, the congregation is not predominantly black. Yes, our worship is lively. No, there are no chandeliers. One fellow whose wife attends a Bible study in my home made a sarcastic remark about religious fanatics and threw in a couple of comments about Jerry Falwell for the same price. Frank and I smiled, and a few others chuckled a bit nervously. I asked the unsuspecting fellow if he knew what a fanatic is, and he sheepishly shook his head.

"A fanatic is anybody who loves God more than you do!" I said. He cocked his head, looking a bit amused and a bit arrested. His wife grinned widely, grateful that for once, her sarcastic, corporate husband didn't have a ready answer. It grew a bit quiet on the deck, and scattered conversations gradually moved to suburbia's top ten topics.

As Frank and I walked home that Sunday night, I reflected upon our own expressions of worship and praise to a living God. I recalled the neighbors lifting their hands in victory at the climax of a golf championship. We lift our hands to God who is victorious over sin and death. We win!

I recalled the students running out of Columbine High School lifting their hands to show that they were unarmed and the aggressors in Kosovo eventually lifting their hands in defeat. We lift our hands to God to show that we surrender—that we give up our rights in order to be His. I recalled our three precious children as toddlers lifting their hands and arms when they were tired and wanted to be picked up and held. We lift our hands to God to show Abba Father that we are yet needy children who desire His embrace, the warmth of His breast, the safety of His lap. I recalled my years in the classroom and the zeal on the faces of those who knew the answers to my questions. They lifted their hands high and proudly, hoping to be called upon.

We lift our hands high and proudly for we are a chosen generation, a royal priesthood, a holy people set apart, and we deeply hope to be called upon because we have the answer and His name is Jesus. Are we fanatics? The Lord will be the judge of that.

So I want men everywhere to pray with holy hands lifted up to God, free from sin and anger and resentment.

—1 Timothy 2:8 (TLB)

23

Enemy Lice

It was the news that every parent dreads. Of course, I blamed myself and wondered if I could have done more. Could I have prevented it from happening? Would there be long-term scars? Would the children eventually resent me or harbor any anger? How I wish I had more knowledge and experience before the crisis arose, but life has a way of turning up surprises, for the good and bad (this was bad). On a humid afternoon in May, I retrieved the mail and was drawn to a letter from the children's elementary school. It was a letter from the principal. I took a deep breath and opened the envelope slowly.

Dear Parent/Guardian:

It has always been our concern to promote quality health of the students in our school and to control and manage communicable diseases. Head lice have been discovered in your child's classroom. Although head lice do not transmit diseases, they are, nevertheless, a nuisance and can cause intense itching and discomfort. Head lice need not carry any stigma. This condition is nothing to be embarrassed about. Anyone, regardless of personal hygiene, can contract head lice. Please check your child's head closely for head lice or the small white nits that look like dandruff (they do not brush off easily). It takes a special, fine-toothed comb to remove nits. If you should find head lice on your child, please seek treatment and notify the school immediately. Your cooperation will help us keep this situation under control.

Sincerely,

Mrs. Hunter

Lice? Surely, our children could not have lice! They wash and brush and bathe and floss every day! I clip their finger and toenails twice a month. I buy Oxy 5 for my daughter, and my son had begun to use deodorant before church and soccer games. I use Clean Shower, Pine Sol, Cinch, and Pledge, and I never water any of them down! I wash clothes with Ultra Tide, Clorox 2, and Downy. We use Dove soap and Pantene shampoo. How could anybody in this house have lice? How could there be an infestation in our very place of refuge? How could the principal send home such an accusatory, shaming letter? It might as well have said:

Dear Slacker,

We desire to promote quality health in our school even if you don't do the same in your home. Creepy crawlies have been discovered on the head of a child whose mother probably watches too much daytime television. Although head lice do not transmit diseases, they can grow quite large and crawl into your child's ears, causing brain damage and a love for MTV. Head lice have always carried a stigma. Most people don't talk about it since there is so much shame and embarrassment associated with the topic. Children of perfect mothers never contract head lice. Good mothers would never allow such a thing to happen to their precious offspring. Please check your child's head, neck, ears, nostrils, and socks closely for these little bugs. Also keep an eye open for the tiny larva eggs that could hatch at any moment, thereby creating a whole new colony on your child's skull. If and when you sight the white oval sacs, apply the fine-toothed comb one hundred times and be prepared to become your child's worst enemy as you pull that minuscule thing across your child's scalp, pulling out her hair along with the nits.

We know you're never going to let us know if you find lice on your kid's head, but remember—we'll find the little pests ourselves if we have to. Please do your job so we won't have to. We're not here for disease control! You can find RID and Nix in aisle five at the local supermarket. Remember, every louse is a no-good, dirty louse. Good luck and go get 'em!

Sincerely,

Mrs. Head Hunter

I paced a bit and then stationed myself at the front door, prepared to greet the troops and review the battle plan. It was 4:01. As usual, the three of them came marching around the curve, looking happy but hungry, backpacks in tow. As they approached the mailbox, they could see the anxious look on my face and their chatter became hushed. My sensitive, discerning son Jordan seemed concerned.

"What's a matta, Ma? Why d'ya look so serious? Is everything okay?"

"I'm not sure if everything is okay. Everybody bend over." Jordan looked shocked.

"Are you going to paddle us out here on the driveway? I promise I'll make my bed tomorrow."

"No, silly, I just have to check something."

The three of them complied, and after a thorough survey in the bright sunlight, I hesitantly conceded that lice did indeed exist in Capri's hair. (It was her first-grade classroom in which the initial case was discovered.) We all got in the car and drove directly to aisle five.

I washed, soaked, rinsed, and rewashed her hair. She was patient as she lay upon the kitchen counter for ninety minutes with her head hanging awkwardly in the sink, and she only cried a little when I pulled that wretched comb through her hair. I stripped her bed and put all of her stuffed animals in airtight bags on the deck, along with pillows, shams, and dolls. I opened all the windows and sprayed enough lice killer to remove them from the county. I turned her brightly colored bedding into pastels by washing everything twice in hot water.

Capri slept well that night, but not I. When I finally dropped into bed after four hours of laundering, wiping, and vacuuming every inch of her bedroom, I had visions of lice-capades gliding across my head. Naturally, I was quite pleased with the fact that I had nipped those nits in the bud. Imagine my reaction when Paris, who was twelve years old at that time, came home with an itchy head the next day. We returned to aisle five and the saga was repeated. This time, the girls slept on towels until I was sure that the pests were banished once and forever. Paris's hair is longer and thicker than Capri's. The combing procedure alone lasted more than two hours and destroyed any warm feelings she had for me. Three days later, I declared the house lice-free and claimed victory. Fortunately, Jordan was never invaded. I wondered how his sisters would look in crew cuts for the summer.

My children wanted to know where lice come from and if and why God made them. They also wanted to know how products that kill lice can be safe for humans. Capri wanted to know when she can have her stuffed animals back, and Paris wanted to know if there's a lice vaccination. Jordan wanted to know if I can shave his head once a week for prevention, and my husband Frank wanted to know how two lice treatments can add up to three digits. I'd much rather explain why the sky is blue.

To you, O Lord, I lift up my soul; in you I trust, O my God. Do not let me be put to shame, nor let my enemies triumph over me.

—Psalm 25:1-2 (NIV)

24

Fathers Needed: Apply in Person

Washington, D.C., has an amazing number of conferences, coalitions, convocations, caucuses, ceremonies, conventions, seminars and expos. This must be the place where they coined the phrase "talking heads." After all, this is the land of free speech, and so it is fitting that the nation's capital is a bastion of such activity. Because of my husband's work with children of prisoners, Frank and I were invited to attend the National Summit on Fatherhood. It was the second gathering of its kind and was sponsored by the National Fatherhood Initiative, a nonprofit secular organization. The roster of men who served as Summit cochairs was extremely impressive: Gore, Powell, Lott, Gingrich, Gephardt, Nunn, Bennett, Armey, Bradley, Kemp (you get the picture). The task force membership roster read like a list of *Who's Who* in the congressional, senatorial, and gubernatorial realm. The financial supporters ranged from Anheuser-Busch (they love fathers) to Dick and Betsy DeVos (they love Jesus and Amway—in that order).

We heard from many speakers during the twelve-hour event. The then-soon-to-be ex-Mayor Marion Barry welcomed everyone to his city, and George Gallup recited lots of statistics. We heard experts from the civic sector, the health sector, the religious sector, the entertainment sector, and the business sector. The luncheon keynote was delivered by then Vice President Al Gore (much less stiff in person). I learned that he attended divinity school after Harvard and before law school. I also learned that he was late to an important meeting with a head of state because it was the Gores' turn to provide snacks for the soccer team after a game that went into double overtime. (I admired that.)

Regardless of race, faith, age, or political orientation, all of the speakers seemed to agree on one thing: Fatherhood in America is in trouble—big trouble. And that means our children are in trouble. One half of all babies born to married couples will see their parents divorce. Substantiated reports from the inner cities tell of crime and social pathology caused by what the experts now call "father absence." Children who grow up without a father in the home are more likely to fail in school, to live in poverty, to use drugs, to become sexually active at an early age, and to display antisocial behavior. Approximately 70 percent of juveniles who are incarcerated grew up without a father at home. Children from broken families are thirty times more likely to suffer health problems than children living with both parents!

And lest you suburbanites begin to feel insulated from all the problems "in the hood," be warned that the most prevalent form of father absence isn't in the inner city. It's in families where fathers are present but not involved in their children's lives. Dr. Robert Coles (author of *The Moral Intelligence of Children* and *The Spiritual Life of Children*) asserts that fathers are all too prone to the "teddy bear syndrome." To quell the guilt, they pacify their children with things instead of time. These fathers are married to their work, and they have little or no interaction with their children when they get home. For all the jokes about a man's domination of the TV remote and the computer mouse—it's no laughing matter. When is the last time you turned off the TV in order to have a conversation, play a board game, or hold a family devotional time? Promise Keepers never intended to be merely a fuzzy warm field trip to a stadium or a memorable media event, but aimed instead for a change in behavior, a better way of life.

As of late, the trouble in our suburbs seems to be more severe than the trouble in our cities. The epidemic of school shootings is proof of that. Columbine, Colorado; Pearl, Mississippi; Paducah,

Kentucky; Jonesboro, Arkansas; Springfield, Oregon; Richmond, Virginia—these hardly sound like places where children need to fear for their lives. A father's (and mother's) love, guidance, and discipline are paramount in the moral rearing of a child. The shame of the parents of those boys who have killed teachers and classmates is the shame of a society that has turned away from God and moral absolutes. We all share in the shame. These tragic incidents have left many dozens of people dead or wounded, and millions ask what went wrong. Naturally, several of the summit's speakers attempted to explain what went wrong and what will go wrong next week and next month and how we should spend more tax dollars and create more programs to make it right. As believers, we are well aware of the only way things will be made right.

After dinner, the National Summit on Fatherhood concluded with the presentation of four "Father of the Year" awards. (Frank felt he should receive one, but I reminded him that pride comes before the fall.) One went to Tom Selleck, a nice guy (and quite handsome). One went to Evander Holyfield, Heavyweight Boxing Champion. One went to Mike Singletary, a former linebacker of the Chicago Bears. Mike boldly told the audience that a father who doesn't worship a holy God can never be a father who will truly impact his children for the good. (Go, Mike!)

The fourth award went to a noncelebrity named Joe from Elmira, New York. This large, muscular man could easily pass for one of Singletary's line mates. His blond flattop made him look a bit ominous, but that first impression melted away when he spoke. Joe is a police sergeant. Sometimes he fills in for his pastor at the local Christian Missionary Alliance church. He donates a lot of time to his community, and he is obviously a well-liked guy in Elmira. We had the privilege of sitting with Joe and his wife at the luncheon earlier in the day. He spoke of his faith and his love for God and for foster children. What I will never forget about Joe was how he beamed when he talked about his daughters—five of them. Like every proud papa, Joe pulled out his wallet and presented me with a short stack of photos. The one on top was of his oldest daughter who is turning twelve. She had her father's blond hair, blue eyes, and small nose. The next few photos were of four beautiful angels ranging from ages five to ten. They were four African-American girls who had all been in long-term foster care. Jesus told Joe and his wife to adopt them, and with the support and counsel of both black and white members of the community, Joe did just that.

Joe from Elmira wasn't the most articulate speaker that day. He didn't quote famous men and never expounded upon sociological theories on the successes and failures of men who happen to also be fathers. But Joe from Elmira will be remembered for something else. His life spoke a loud and clear message. Words pale in comparison to the moisture in his eyes as he passed around the photos of his kids. May the Lord strengthen our fathers, and may more men like Joe be willing to stand in the gap and become fathers to the fatherless.

Fathers face an overwhelming task in raising their children and grandchildren in this fast-paced, bumpy ride called life. Men can seek (and women can encourage them to seek) outside guidance. Consider a men's accountability group at church, a breakfast club of Christian dads, or an older mentor who can become a prayer and counseling partner. And it's never too late to begin a family devotion time. For more excellent resources for men (and for the women who want to encourage them), consult the following books:

The Four Pillars of a Man by Stu Weber
The Father Book by Frank Minirth
God of My Father by Larry and Lawrence Crabb
As Iron Sharpens Iron by Howard and Bill Hendricks
Things We Wish We Had Said by Tony and Bart Campolo
How to Be A Hero to Your Kids by Josh McDowell
When Men Think Private Thoughts by George MacDonald
Tender Warrior by Stu Weber

And you, fathers, do not provoke your children to wrath, but bring them up in the training and admonition of the Lord.

—Ephesians 6:4 (NKJV)

25

Homework Helper

ome women dread the summer months and the unavoidable protests of boredom. No such thing at the Lofaro home. We (the children and I) stay up late and sleep in late and watch cartoons and dress by noon. It's "every man for himself" at breakfast and lunch. We read new books and rent old movies and finish puzzles. We take day trips and overnight trips and beach trips. We have sports camp and church camp and VBS. We're regulars at the local pool and occasionally spend the day at a water park. When it's really hot outside, we go bowling or stroll through the mall. When Frank walks in at 6:30, there's not a homework assignment in sight. If we're not there, he dials my cell phone and brings deli to the pool or tells me what to pick up for grilling. Most summer nights culminate with ice cream and *I Love Lucy* reruns. Summertime . . . and the livin' is easy. I really love it.

When the school year ends, it is never a moment too soon. Homework, quizzes, tests, science projects, book reports—they exhaust me! And there's more: field trips, extra help, conferences, PTA meetings, fund-raisers, lunches, cupcakes, elections, plays, choir, band, Teacher Appreciation Week, Secretary's Day, show-and-tell. Where does a mother go to resign? How about a leave of absence? A day off?

My husband and I share very different philosophies regarding homework and study habits. He is quite relentless about the subject of homework. Can you spell B-E-A-R? When the kids are sent home with notes or if their grades drop, he glares at me and invariably delivers the now infamous speech: "Ellie, we have arranged for you not to have to work outside of the home so that you could fully focus on the children. I'm not concerned when there is no dinner or the laundry is backed up, but you MUST make their homework your top priority." That speech always produces an array of emotional responses—some I am unable to mention here—suffice it to say the heart can be unlovely.

In Frank's perfect world, he would stroll in at 6:30 to find me gleefully rotating to each child to correct spelling, review math for-mulas, and assist with special projects. He had our second grader writing rough drafts for her book summary every night. Poor thing, I pray she doesn't end up in therapy. Jordan is a slop-py, forgetful, perfectly normal boy, but Frank warns him that his present work habits will ruin his entire future, personally and professionally, and that he may be a candidate for welfare if he doesn't shape up and step in line. Paris is completely self-moti-vated, which is appropriate for the secondary school years. Nonetheless, Frank has decided she must read one additional novel a week during seventh grade to enhance her verbal skills for the college-entrance exams (which she will eventually take in five years).

So, top management sends down orders, and middle manage-ment is supposed to carry them out, but now I understand why the workers sometimes revolt. I can't blame them, and I have often warned Frank of the backlash he may face twenty years down the road. (Our kids are afraid Frank will assign homework to the grand-children.) It's very tough being in the middle. Paris became very frustrated with her "extracurricular" reading load. She let off some steam. "I can't believe Daddy is making us do so much work!"

Experts say you should not contradict your spouse in front of the children or management in front of labor—but I'm only human. "Me neither! It's getting out of hand. I've had enough!" I was putting finishing touches on Jordan's volcano, and the plaster was drying quickly on my eyelashes. Jordan chimed in.

"Mom, I can't take it anymore. After this, you have to help me with my math."

"I don't understand your math, Jordan. It's all different now."

"But Mom, you were a teacher!"

"I taught English. I hated math—still do."

"Well, then you have to help me write my book report."

"Jordan, I already went to fifth grade. I passed fifth grade. I'm not doing fifth grade again. Do your own book report!" He had Frank's *look* in his eyes.

"Dad said you have to help me. *Priorities*—remember?"

Capri joined the bandwagon. "Mommy, I have too much weading! Can you please wead me this book? I love how you wead!"

I felt that "Calgon, take me away," sensation suddenly come over me. I don't recall getting help with anything school related during *my* childhood. My mother packed our lunches, laid out clean (and pressed) clothes, and occasionally rubbed on Vicks VapoRub or calamine lotion—depending on the season. Not once do I remember her sitting at the kitchen table to review math problems or research the Middle Ages. I called her on Mother's Day. My fears were confirmed.

"Hi, Ma, it's me. Happy Mother's Day!"

"Thank you, Lella. You're one of my greatest gifts."

"Thanks Ma . . . listen Ma . . . did you ever help me with my homework?"

"No, no. You were so smart, you never needed help."

"Were the boys also smart? You never helped them either."

"The boys turned out just fine."

"Were you involved with the PTA?"

"Yes, of course, I paid the dues every year."

"Did you go on any field trips?"

"No, honey, only the pushy mothers went."

"Did you ever help me with a special project? I don't remember having any art materials in the house."

"Ellie, don't be silly. You kids were in one of the best school districts on Long Island."

"But Ma, we were *never* allowed to have glitter, Silly Putty, or

Magic Markers in the house. My projects were shoe boxes colored with crayons. We were deprived!"

"Everything you needed was at school. There was no reason to mess the house."

"Why didn't you read to me? You know—the Dick and Jane books."

"Oh, Lella—what's the matter with you? I didn't read out loud because I didn't want you to get confused. Thirty-five years ago, my accent was still very strong. Be thankful."

"How come you never checked my homework?"

"You were perfect. What was there to check? Happy Mother's Day, Booboolla. Except for moving my grandchildren three hundred miles away, you're *still* perfect."

"Thank you, Mother. So are you."

Our culture encourages us to blame others for our pain. Parents, friends, old lovers. Science points to genetics, DNA, predisposition. You are what you are because that's what your father was or that's what your mother did. Even some Christians feel a certain amount of exoneration by pointing out the "sins of their forefathers." The living God has decreed that the old things have passed away and all things (including us) have been made new. In Christ I am a new creation. The Father I must emulate is perfect. That pretty much cancels out my list of excuses. I'll try to do better with homework next year.

*S*o let us try to do what makes peace and helps one another.

—Romans 14:19 (NCV)

26

Fear Not

It seems to me that the majority of the people who live in and around Washington, D.C., either work for the government or for a company with government contracts. I think the rest work in telecommunications and Internet firms. Like the government agencies, many computer companies are also known by three initials: EDS, NEC, and ADT are right across the street from ATF, CIA, and EPA. We also host America Online, Microsoft, Computer Associates, Apple, Wang, and Oracle. I am not one to be particularly interested in the world of computers. I am not proud of that. It's just a fact. Of course, I understand the importance of computers and the role they play in our everyday lives. Well, let me retract that last statement. I *thought* I understood the role they play in our everyday lives. That is, up until Easter Sunday 1998. At Easter Sunday dinner, my understanding of the importance of computers and the role they play in our everyday lives was forever altered.

The morning seemed glorious, with a cloudless blue sky, budding trees, and blooming flowers. The morning service was a fount to the thirsty; the children's rendition brought tears, and the lilies filled the sanctuary with the sweetness of Christ. A beautiful nylon purple flag with a gold cross hung outside the front door of our home. The kids colored eggs the day before, and the Honey Baked Ham was ready to be heated. I felt so thankful to God to be able to open our home to eleven people who (like hundreds of thousands) find themselves away from family during a holiday.

The children each read from the Scriptures, we reflected on eternal life, and Frank lifted a prayer and gave a priestly blessing. The ham was presented (I added pineapple rings on top—very gourmet), the side dishes were served, and the warm rolls were passed around the table. I served thinly sliced turkey breast to my friend Miriam, a Messianic Jew who keeps Kosher and wants to know why Christians celebrate a Jewish Messiah by eating a ham. (I told Miriam I'd get back to her on that one.) The dining room actually looked like a Norman Rockwell scene, and I felt pleased to be the hostess. The adults took turns sharing ten-minute testimonies as the seven children giggled in the kitchen, attempting to eat the toasted marshmallow topping off the sweet potatoes. They were excused to play in the yard and the adult conversation turned toward the topic of computers.

John is an expert programmer, Ann is an expert analyst, and Robert is an expert sales associate. Although they had not known each other well, they formed a powerful alliance and spoke with great computer authority as they proceeded to expound upon the role of computers in the new millennium—more specifically—on January 1, 2000.

JOHN: Complete havoc will break loose just after the stroke of midnight. The most far-reaching ramifications cannot be fathomed.

ANN: That's correct. It's no secret that come Millennium Eve, computers everywhere will be crashing faster than the Indonesian rupiah.

ROBERT: It's true. Officials have only fixed 35 percent of the most vital federal mainframes and won't have time before December 31, 1999, to prevent all the 5,100 remaining computers from deciding it's 1900, not 2000.

JOHN: You'll wake up on January 1 without any heat or electricity. Those systems are completely automated by computer chips.

ANN: You'll pick up the phone to call your neighbor, but the phone line will be dead.

Now they had my complete attention. "Computer chips?" I asked.

"Absolutely," she retorted.

ROBERT: You'll get dressed and go down to start your car, but it won't start.

"Computer chips?" I asked again, this time more incredulously. He nodded. "That sounds crazy. I never saw a computer anything in my car."

He looked at me with pity. "It's in a small box under the driver's seat to the right."

JOHN: The food in your fridge will rot (more unruly chips!), and the supermarket will have similar problems, not to mention that your money will suddenly be worthless, because everyone will make withdrawals, and there won't be cash left, and the bank records will all be erased.

ANN: Financial transactions will be delayed, social security records will be erased, airline flights grounded, fuel pumps shut down, and national defense seriously affected. Let's not even get into people passing through toll booths or those caught in an elevator!

ROBERT: Major raids could occur, and food shipments could come to a halt because of computerized railways. People with a major surplus of anything will need a gun.

Frank made a mildly sarcastic remark, and my mother chided him for being an arrogant, smug American. She reminded him of the steel bunker her father built in 1943 and her childhood memory of a brush with Nazi tanks. (She threw a "dirt bomb" at one when she was nine.) She reminded him of the wealthy Europeans who burned valuable artwork, furniture, and clothing to produce heat for their children. She then reminded him of a few other things as only a mother-in-law could.

JOHN: Remember, there were two thousand years between Adam and Abraham, two thousand years between Abraham and Jesus—and here comes the close of another two thousand—so this could be it.

The temperature hit seventy-five degrees and the sky remained cloudless, but it got a bit gloomy around the dining room table. A missionary friend brought some eternal perspective to the conversation; an older woman reminded everyone that no one knows the day or the hour. Frank excused himself from the table and invited the men to follow him downstairs to catch the end of the PGA Masters tournament. He praised the dinner, kissed me on the forehead, and gave me the "I need a nap" look. A few families joined us for dessert (which was heavily "sprinkled" with end-times innuendo), and five hours later, I dropped my tired body into the bed where my well-rested husband was already fast asleep.

Thoughts of the dinner conversation swirled through my sleepy head. I elbowed Mr. Wonderful. "Frank, Frank, wake up. I told you I never liked computers! What are we going to do if any of what they said is true? What are you thinking? What is your plan? Where should we be on December 31, 1999?"

He rolled over, lifted his head, and answered sincerely, "We'll go to Disney World."

"We *can't* go to Disney World—it's completely booked. What's your next plan?"

"We'll move to Montana, buy a few guns, and stock up on Campbell's soup."

My knight in shining armor patted me on the head. "It'll be all right, honey. Go to sleep." He then rolled over into unconsciousness. I stared at the bedroom ceiling for a long while that night and pondered many things. I took a deep sigh, curled up on my side, and reflected on the meaning of Easter.

People today are afraid—especially of death and dying. People want to live. Some want to live longer, some want to live better, and some want to live forever. Consider what took place at the cross and the empty tomb. The power of Easter morning forever defeated the power of death. I am so thankful that God had forever in mind when He rolled the stone away. And I'm so relieved that our good-byes are not final. I slept well that night.

Do not be afraid that some plan conceived behind closed doors will be the end of you. Do not fear anything except the Lord Almighty. He alone is the Holy One. If you fear him, you need fear nothing else. He will keep you safe.

—Isaiah 8:12-14 (NLT)

27

Sweet and Sour

Of all the holidays we celebrate in America, it seems to me that Thanksgiving has been the least adulterated. Oh sure, we see greeting cards and turkey-shaped cocktail napkins, but it never really gets much worse than that. Nobody expects presents, and there are no make-believe characters that appear, and the children don't hunt for anything, and Tom Turkey never takes on a superhero persona. What a relief! When all is said and done, Thanksgiving is widely acknowledged as a day to feast, rest, and give thanks. But to whom do Americans give thanks? Or, in some cases, to what?

In our self-serving, if-it-feels-good-do-it, look-out-for-number-one culture, many people are thankful only to themselves. They take full credit for every comfort, every accomplishment, every acquisition. Their credo is "Do what's good for yourself every chance you get. Don't inconvenience yourself for anybody, and keep a running tally when you do. Remember that you only get to the top through your own sweat and blood, and that's also how you'll stay there. Staying there will be very tough because there are people just waiting to trip you up and watch you fall on your face. Watch your back."

Others are thankful for their circumstances and good fortune (knock on wood). They glance at the hunger telethons and "feel so lucky" to have a pantry full of food. They read about the rising number of AIDS-related deaths and feel so lucky not to have to deal with such a plague. They hear about a neighbor with cancer and thank their lucky stars not to have it. They learn about the adulterous co-worker and wonder if his rejected wife drove him to it. These people think they're the lucky ones and hope luck won't run out.

Then there are the solid citizens. These are the law-abiding folks who work hard, pay taxes on time, and give to charity. They buy houses in good neighborhoods with good schools where their children will grow up and go to good colleges so they can get good jobs. Then their children can attract the right kind of people in hopes of finding a good mate and buying a house in a good neighborhood. Often (but not always), elitism, racism, and ethnocentricity hide their ugly heads in these "good" neighborhoods.

People who are thankful for their ability to "make it on their own," people who are thankful for "their good luck," people who are thankful to "live on the right side of the tracks." As Christians, we should not desire to fit comfortably into any of these categories. Yet, my discomfort is palpable even as these words flow from head to paper. Has self-sufficiency and pride tainted my relationships? Yes. Have I confused good health and material blessing with God's stamp of approval? Yes. Are there traces of bigotry within me? Yes. I have so often been arrogant in my estimation of others. God help me.

I "helped God" in Haiti once but never on a regular basis in the city slum. I sent clothes to the homeless on several occasions but have never visited them. I wrote to my brother when he was in prison but felt so relieved he was on the west coast. I shared the gospel hundreds of times, but far too many of those encounters took place without a genuine Christlike love for the hearer. I have struggled to like people who don't like me. I try to forgive those who have offended me, but I have not forgotten. I have given my life to proclaim one Christ over one body but have regretfully allowed myself to be sidetracked by tunnel-visioned, modern-day Pharisees. I am so deeply grateful that God's mercies are new every morning. My heart overflows with thanks for what He accomplished on the cross.

For what are you thankful? If you own just one Bible, you are more fortunate than one third of the world's population, which does not have access to even one. If you have fairly good health, you are healthier than the one million people who will not survive the week. If you have ample food, clothing, and a solid roof over your head, then you are richer than three-fourths of the people on the planet. If you have savings in the bank, money in your wallet and spare change around the house, you are among the top 8 percent of the world's wealthy. This information is not meant to make us feel guilty about being comfortable, but it should cause us to think about our grumbling. We should be shouting thanks from our rooftops!

That is not to say an abiding faith in God ensures good health, material blessing, and the absence of heartache. Jesus said we would have trouble—He said to count on it. And He didn't mean babies with colic, broken mufflers, or torn nylons! Tell the Christians in Sudan that believers don't suffer. Tell the Christians who are steeped in grief and agonizing in deep depression that believers don't suffer. Tell the woman from church whose husband just left her after thirty-two years that believers don't suffer. Tell the godly neighbor who just lost both breasts to that plague called cancer that believers don't suffer. Tell the precious family who had their bright and beautiful teenager so suddenly taken that believers don't suffer. The lonely and afraid, the worried and bankrupt, the terminally ill—these storms of life have caused many people to lose their way.

A medieval monk once remarked, "We fall down, we get up. We fall down, we get up. A saint is just a sinner who falls down and gets up." Our sin is not in falling, but rather in not getting back up. Isn't that really the essence of faith? As long as we find ourselves on earth's soil, the battle will rage. When I first professed my devotion to Christ, life was a bed of roses, a bowl of cherries, and a cool glass of lemonade. Since 1972, I have grown in stature, wisdom, and knowledge (as every healthy child should). Over the years the Lord has allowed (and sometimes arranged) for me to encounter the thorns, the pits, and some very bitter rinds. Did He love me more back then? Not at all. I believe He trusts me with more now—the sour as well as the sweet.

And so we find reason to thank Him no matter the circumstances. Whether you find yourself in a season of abundance or need, joy or sorrow, celebration or mourning, be sure to give thanks, to press on, and to get back up when you fall. Give thanks to God solely because He is God. Years ago, my old friend Margaret Becker penned a song titled "For the Love of You."[1] She eloquently expresses a desire to love God with pure motives.

> Been searching deep inside me to find some hidden clues
> About my motivation for loving You.
> I know there is the obvious; Your blessings and Your peace.
> But what if all your benefits were to suddenly decrease?
> Way beyond the things I know I will receive
> I want my motivation for loving You to be
> For the love, for the love of You, not for what it brings.
> For the love, for the love of You, let me do all things;
> Not for what You'll do—but just for the love of You.

Oh, that I could love God for the sheer pleasure and privilege of loving Him.

> *I* have told you these things, so that in me you may have peace. In this world you will have trouble. But take heart! I have overcome the world.
> —John 16:33 (NIV)

28

Dog Dodging

When my daughter Paris turned ten, she announced it was the worst birthday of her entire life. Paris is a lovely, well-adjusted, bright, communicative child. But this particular birthday brought out a side of her I didn't know existed. I need to take you back to her fifth birthday.

"Mommy, I want a dog for my birthday."

"Now, sweetie, a dog is a big responsibility, and you are only five, and your little brother, Jordan, is only three, and this baby in my belly is coming out any minute. (Capri arrived the very next day.) Mommy can't take care of a new baby and a new dog all at the same time."

She looked at me with a combination of disappointment and compassion and seemed to accept my explanation. "How about when I'm bigger?"

The child obviously was not backing down, so I proceeded to make a promise I thought she would surely forget. (Men are not the only ones who struggle to be good promise keepers.)

"Paris, when you turn ten, we will get a dog for your birthday."

"You promise, Mommy?"

"I promise, honey."

It seemed like a safe enough thing to say at the time, but who ever knew she would turn ten and develop such sharp verbal and reasoning skills, along with a keen memory? The child clearly bided her time. She has held many dogs through the years. She has stared through the windows of puppy shops. She has checked dog books out of the library. She even picked dog movies at Blockbuster. But, did she ever again mention the subject of wanting a dog? No. Never. Not once. That is, not until exactly one week before her tenth birthday.

It was early Saturday morning. Frank had already left for his weekly ritual at the office, and I was in a deep, well-deserved sleep, which was abruptly interrupted by deliberate, rhythmic, heavy breathing four inches from my face. When I forced my eyelids to open, six eyeballs stared back. The child with the largest eyeballs spoke first. She was no longer a trusting, pliable five-year-old.

"Mother, you made a *very* serious promise, and you taught us that character and integrity and trust are *very* important, and you promised I would get a dog for my tenth birthday, and I hope you don't break your promise, because that would be *very* bad for our relationship, and also Jordan and Capri would learn a *very* bad lesson."

As if they had rehearsed this indignant demonstration, the other two folded their arms, scowled, leaned closer to my sleepy face and simultaneously grunted, "That's right!"

I groped for words. "Paris, there are times we will let you down, but you should *always* trust us. We're your parents. There are many reasons why we cannot buy a dog."

"Name them, Mom."

"Dogs are a lot of work. Dogs get fleas and ticks."

"So? I had lice and everything turned out all right."

"Dogs drool, slobber, chew furniture, and shed hair all over the house."

"I'll vacuum *every day.*"

"You don't even brush your teeth every day! Are you telling me you're going to walk the dog, wash the dog, watch for ticks, and vacuum up all the hair every day?"

"Yes, Mom, I promise."

"Be careful what you promise." (I should know.)

"Mom, all my friends have dogs, and all the neighbors have dogs."

"I'm not interested in what the neighbors have. *Who* has a dog?"

"The Simons have a dog."

"Mrs. Simon is very lonely because Mr. Simon is retired and golfs every day."

"The Corcorans have a dog."

"Mrs. Corcoran feels bad that Jonathan is an only child, and they bought a dog as a playmate. You are so fortunate to have a brother and a sister."

"The Andersons have a dog."

"That's because they have six kids, and Mrs. Anderson uses the dog to keep the younger children busy."

Jordan finally interjected in frustration. "The Felders have two dogs, a gerbil, a hamster, a cat, and two parrots. Those kids are soooo lucky!"

"Lucky? Their house smells like a petting zoo. Thank the Lord you have a mother who cares enough to say no."

Capri was next to chime in. "Dear Jesus, give us a mommy who cares enough to say yes." Even though I was still lying down, my heart dropped to my feet.

"Listen you guys, I am very, very sorry. I know I made a promise, but I should *not* have made it. Forgive me, I was wrong. Sometimes promises are broken for good reasons."

Paris's eyes narrowed. "Name one."

"We travel too often to own a dog."

"Mom, haven't you ever heard of kennels?"

"Yes, but it's cruel to put a dog in a kennel. Dogs have feelings you know."

"Yeah, Ma, we know. Kids have feelings too."

The three of them stared at me with the most dejected, pathetic expressions I have ever seen on their beautiful faces. I tried to bring some ray of hope.

"Paris, you WILL have a dog someday."

"When?"

"When you're twenty."

"You promise?"

"Absolutely."

Are there any colleges that allow dogs on campus? I'll gladly supply all the food.

> *A*nd since you know that he cares, let your language show it. Don't add words like "I swear to God" to your own words. Don't show your impatience by concocting oaths to hurry up God. Just say yes or no. Just say what is true. That way, your language can't be used against you.
>
> —James 5:12 (*The Message*)

29

The Maiden Voyage

o you remember the movie titled *The Four Seasons?* It starred Alan Alda and Carol Burnett. The opening scene spans a gorgeous alcove in some Caribbean bay and zooms in on an anchored sailing yacht. Alda and Burnett are married, in love, in midlife bliss. They have chartered an impressive vessel and are obviously having the vacation of a lifetime with two other couples. They are all close friends who have known one another for many years and watched each other's children grow. Frank and I were engaged when this film was released back in 1981, and my romantic husband-to-be decided then that we, too, would someday sail the Caribbean. Frank's prophecy came to pass.

Please allow me to state from the outset that I do not wish to be perceived as a murmurer, a spoiled brat, nor a malcontent with an ungrateful heart. I obviously survived the week on the Caribbean waters and have recovered well enough to tell about it. Your prayers for my continued healing would be deeply appreciated. I would have activated a few prayer chains during my time away, but no phones were available. When we finally hit dry land, I was partially drugged by the motion-sickness pills that kicked in three days late.

I suppose I should have known I was in for some trouble when the charter agreement came in the mail. It arrived on a frostbitten day in February, so thoughts of escape to balmy breezes temporarily distracted me from the fine print in the contract.

"Frank, don't you think three thousand dollars is awfully expensive? After all, we're working for a ministry now." Frank looked puzzled.

"Honey, I've been working very hard with no break and besides, remember we're three couples. A thousand dollars is actually reasonable for seven nights of lodging and three meals a day and unlimited snorkeling and scuba diving." I looked puzzled.

"Scuba diving? Who's going scuba diving? Do I look like Jacques Cousteau?"

I continued to peruse the charter agreement. The insurance portion caught my attention:

> The owner of the charter and his insurance under-
> writers accept no responsibility for accidents,
> injuries, or death due to swimming or the use of
> snorkels, masks, or scuba equipment. Neither the
> vessel, nor the owner, or his agents are liable for
> any bodily injury or death related to water skiing,
> spinnaker flying, the vessel's dinghy, or the out-
> board motor.

"Oh, great, Frank, I feel much better now. I don't have to worry about sharks—the outboard motor will attack me! I could see the headline now: SUBURBAN MOTHER DROWNED BY WILD DINGHY.

D day arrived, and we traveled from Washington, D.C., to San Juan, Puerto Rico. There we met one couple from Denver and another from Boston. Unlike the three couples in the movie, we were linked by the personal/professional relationships between the men. I had only briefly met these two women in passing, but I had a feeling we would know each other more intimately by the end of the week.

We boarded a small prop plane and landed on Tortola, one of the British Virgin Islands. A short taxi ride brought us to Fort Burt Marina, where we boarded the yacht. I soon learned the word "yacht" denotes any vessel over thirty feet. This one was forty-five feet long and older than we had expected. The name *Lady Luck* was painted on the back (aft?) An omen, I concluded.

The captain and the cook enthusiastically greeted us. The captain was a fine twenty-something gent from South Africa. His blond hair was sun bleached from his head to his toes, and his accent was charming. The cook was a "maiden of the sea" in some respects. No, not the lady on the tuna can but a woman who left Australia at age eighteen and has been job and adventure hopping for twenty years. Her raspy voice and taut skin betrayed that life had hardened her. After getting past the desire to stare at her tattoos, I later discovered that she offered some of the most thought-provoking, heartwarming conversation of our excursion. Alas, the sea has left her worn but wise.

On the first day, we sailed to Beef Island. I wore my neck patch and my motion wristband, and I took a pill, and I prayed (not in that order). Nonetheless, I got pretty sick. I slowly stumbled to the head (toilet in sea lingo). This facility was three feet wide by four feet long, including the bathtub, which was literally a little tub with a hand nozzle. It made airplane bathrooms feel like the Ritz. I sat for a long while, rocked left and right, broke a cold sweat, searched for toilet paper, and gradually became sicker. Depleted of strength, lucid thinking, and balance, I attempted to flush. No such thing on *Lady Luck*. I focused on the directions hanging ten inches from my nose and to my horror, began reading how one should properly "pump" the receptacle. I pumped and rocked and sweated and pumped and rocked and sweated. Surely a Hyatt or Hilton could be found within twenty miles. I wondered if Frank could buy the dumb boat and command the captain to go there.

When I finally emerged perspiring and pale, dinner was being served. It was curried chicken with rice and a vegetable. I have a strong, somewhat emotional aversion to curry. The next night's dinner was covered with hot pepper flakes, and the one after that was drowned in chili sauce. I actually longed for my own bland, pathetic cooking. I concluded that twenty years at sea had seared the cook's taste buds—bless her heart and pass the Pepto-Bismol. I excused myself early and climbed down the hatch and crawled into bed. Well, it wasn't really a bed. I killed an earwig on the way and decided to skip a visit to the head. Personal hygiene no longer ranked as a top priority. Survival did. We soon anchored in a bay and I was rocked into a twelve-hour deep sleep.

The next day, we hiked around a small island, and the day after that, we took a brief scuba lesson from our trusty captain. The peer pressure to go along was unbearable, and I would never have lived down all the stories of what they saw down there. Before I could back out, I was jumping in with full gear. If the weight of the tank didn't drown me, I was sure the awkward fins would. We plunged from the vessel down into the water, just like a bunch of coast guard frogmen. After practicing our hand signals one more time, we descended sixty feet to an old shipwreck—or what was left of it.

The descent was filled with sights too spectacular to describe. The visual utopia was somewhat interrupted by mental meanderings. *Will I run out of oxygen? Will a creature bite my hose? Will an air bubble enter my lungs? How about my brain? Do the little fish think we're big fish? What was the hand signal for popping eardrums? Why did he say not to ascend too quickly? Where's Frank?* I shot a glance ahead and then behind as we passed through the wreck. Frank's tank was caught on what seemed to be a door frame. He looked like a cartoon character as he flapped his fins vigorously while going nowhere. Poor honey. The captain released him, and I was afraid to laugh for fear of swallowing the sea and dying of brain bubbles.

We spent the next two days avoiding the sun and applying large globs of aloe to our burned bodies. We became more comfortable and transparent with one another, thanks to being confined together on a boat. I even got used to the procedures when the captain shouted, "Coming about!" By the fifth day, I also mastered the pumping action down below. It wasn't until our final swim off *Lady Luck* that I learned more about the operation of the head—a topic that held my interest all week. Upon probing the captain a bit, I found out that the pumping action resulted in deposits to the sea. I decided to cut the swim short, climb the ladder quickly, and towel dry myself quite thoroughly.

The final night of our maiden voyage was actually quite perfect. The sunset was breathtaking, the dinner was delectable (we docked and ate out), the public showers were clean and hot, the stars were brilliant, and our final group devotion was very moving. I rocked to sleep in Frank's arms, and there wasn't an earwig in sight.

When I look at the night sky and see the work of your fingers—the moon and the stars you have set in place—what are mortals that you should think of us, mere humans that you should care for us?
—Psalm 8:3-4 (NLT)

30

Snowbound

The Blizzard of '96 . . . I remember it all too well. That's because I kept a journal. I didn't have much else to do that week.

Day 1, Sunday: By 8 am, six fluffy inches of snow had already fallen over the Washington, D.C., tri-state area. Our wonderful children (ages three, six, and eight) greeted us with warm smiles, tight cuddles, and sighs of joy as they piled onto our bed. Frank lifted all the shades, and we gazed into the early morning winter wonderland. The beauty and stillness were mesmerizing. Since all of the church services were canceled, we attempted a simple, shortened version right there in the master bedroom. A Scripture reading, some prayer requests, a song, a prayer—innocent little thoughts from precious hearts, reminding us of our need to be like children. Chef Frank announced that the world's best waffles would be ready in ten minutes. We finished eating breakfast by eleven o'clock and continued to stare out the large bay window next to the kitchen table. It was obviously going to be a pajama day, and I, for one, was quite content with that. It continued to snow heavily throughout the afternoon and into the evening. We played a couple of games and watched *White Christmas* and had wrestling matches in between. Except for the videos, it was probably the closest we've ever come to life on Walton Mountain. Two feet of glorious snow had fallen by evening.

"Good night, Mommy."

"Good night, Paris."

"Good night, Jordan."

"Good night, Daddy."

"Good night, Jordan."

"Good night, Capri."

"Good night, Mommy."

"Good night, Jordan."

"Good night, honey."

I kissed Frank and fell asleep with happy thoughts and a grateful heart.

Day 2, Monday: I woke up to the sound of giggling coming from under my bed. My three-year-old daughter Capri had dressed up like Cinderella and felt quite pleased with herself. I escorted the princess downstairs to find the other two kids working on a big puzzle with little pieces. Frank was reading the Sunday paper, which had been delivered late Saturday night. The fireplace was burning strong, the radio was tuned to jazz, and I managed to cook perfect French toast. While I poured cold milk into the large kettle, I felt thankful that we had two whole gallons in the fridge. Going to the market late Saturday night was a wise idea. The hot cocoa was a big hit that morning, especially since it was covered with minimarshmallows. Frank and the children bundled up to shovel and play in the snow. I read for a while, then made soup and grilled cheese sandwiches. Three hours passed, and the gang reentered, wet, cold and hungry. "Mom, please make us hot cocoa again. We're shivering."

"Coming right up, sweetie." We had a long lunch and some deep conversation (considering their ages). Frank and I noticed how much the years were flying by and how quickly their personalities were developing. By sundown, they were hungry again. I happily served leftovers and noted that how strange it was that we hadn't seen a single plow on the street. We played with some Christmas gifts, watched another favorite film, and hit the sack.

Day 3, Tuesday: I awoke to cries coming from the children's bathroom. Someone had clogged the toilet. As I ran downstairs for the mop, I observed with shock that the street had still not been cleared. "We're only four hours south of New York City. Is it possible there's no snow-removal equipment here?" Frank gave me a *look* as he pulled wads of paper from the toilet.

"Of course there's equipment here. It's not Florida!" A loud thud came from the kitchen, and I ran back downstairs, only to find Jordan's large bowl of milk and cereal now all over the floor. I began to clean it up, only to find wet little puzzle pieces floating with the cereal. The doorbell rang. (The Iceman cometh?) With matted hair, I answered it. It was our neighbor. She has two boys and ran out of milk. Frank handed her an unopened gallon, which left us with less than a quart. She smiled and waved good-bye as she pranced off in her snow-bunny ski suit with my milk.

"Are you crazy? What about *our* kids? They need milk! What will we do?" Frank gave me another *look,* this time one of pity (most likely, for himself). By this time, the spilled cereal had cemented to the floor, and I headed to the basement to find the vacuum. Imagine my horror to find Play-Doh, glitter, beads, and glue mixed together in a 3-D sculpture on the couch. My three-year-old couldn't understand why I didn't feel happy about her latest achievement. The kids went out again, and Frank disappeared into his study. I went on a mission to search and destroy Play Doh pellets. The kids came in sooner than I had expected, and two were crying because of a loose dog that jumped on them. "I'm never goin' outside the rest of my life!" They stood by the fire to get warm and pleaded for hot cocoa. But, you guessed it. No milk left. We ate cold cuts for dinner and drank soda. The day ended as it began—the same toilet overflowed. As I fell into bed feeling quite drained, the flash news bulletin stated that all schools would be closed the rest of the week and would reopen next Tuesday, after the Martin Luther King holiday. *Seven more days of togetherness? Lord, give me strength!*

Day 4, Wednesday: I hadn't slept well, so when the three musketeers jumped on my bed at 7 am, I ordered them to "Get out!" They left the smell of Play-Doh in their wake. Once again, they ate cereal, this time without any milk. I banned all arts and crafts activities, sent the trio out in the snow, did laundry, unloaded the dishwasher, refilled it, and continued to pile garbage in the garage. At 3 pm, one small pickup truck with one small plow cleared one narrow lane down our street. I slept most of the day and went to sleep early while Frank worked on our taxes.

Day 5, Thursday: I sent Frank out for milk, bread, eggs, etc. You know, all the things a woman would want in the house if the world were ending. The car got stuck, so Frank returned home without accomplishing his mission. I did more laundry, changed all the sheets, and let the kids watch cartoons most of the day. They had potato chips for lunch and more dry cereal for dinner. Huge Caterpillar machinery arrived in the neighborhood to displace the many tons of snow in order for us to receive mail as well as garbage collection. The garage was beginning to smell, and I am quite positive that clinical effects of extreme cabin fever were beginning to set in.

Day 6, Friday: The kids were bored from the moment they awoke. My promises as well as my threats seemed meaningless. The temperature had dropped severely, and another foot of snow was expected and began to fall. I threw a coat on over my sweats, got into my car, and skidded all the way to the supermarket. I was not prepared for what I was about to see. Or, shall I say, *not* see? No milk, no bread, no eggs. Not even chicken or beef in any form. They were even out of Spam! What if they were to run out of milk indefinitely? What if the trucks can't get through? What if the Lord returns? An elderly woman mistakenly got on the express line and a mob almost lynched her. Lines stretched from the cashiers to the back wall. I bought a few necessary items, waited in line for seventy-nine minutes, and arrived home to find Frank and the children enjoying hot cocoa. (The snow bunny returned the milk that she had borrowed.) Maybe things weren't as wonderful as they seemed up on Walton Mountain.

Day 7, Saturday: In all, thirty-one inches of snow have fallen on our house this week. Although I *eventually* arrived at a peaceful place of surrender, my frustration did not instantly dissolve. *Eventually* I learned that lesson about not worrying. *Eventually* I saw that Frank used the opportunity of sharing a gallon of milk to also share a cup of faith. *Eventually* I saw the big picture. But I am still a work in progress.

So don't be anxious about tomorrow. God will take care of your tomorrow too. Live one day at a time.
—Matthew 6:34 (TLB)

31

Newsletter Etiquette

Would you believe we received forty-six Christmas newsletters one year? It took me a month, but I read through each and every one. The first one came the Tuesday after Thanksgiving (that woman is too organized), and the last one came the day after Epiphany (more my speed). I squeezed each one into a jumbo, electric-blue paper clip and placed them in a neat pile on top of the master toilet, and well, you know how that goes. My husband and I call it bathroom reading. No allusion to the content of course—it has more to do with time management. I took my time (all of January), but Frank lost interest after number six. He lamented that they all sounded alike and warned that reading for extended periods while sitting on porcelain can be harmful to one's health. Is that true?

Where did my very first Christmas newsletter come from? It was the early seventies, and my cousin Lorraine married a fellow who was serving at a U.S. Naval base in Naples, Italy. Sending an update to loved ones overseas was standard naval wife protocol, and I was quite taken with the concept. I was a high school freshman and thought her life seemed like a romance novel. In the early eighties, I got married, and we began to receive newsletters from friends who had gone to foreign mission fields. Naturally, the newsletters they sent at Christmas tended to have more personal content and an occasional (poor quality) photo from an old copy machine obviously in need of service somewhere in the third world. Everybody's teeth always looked black. By the early nineties, we were only receiving four or five newsletters at Christmas time, but then something happened in 1994 that changed all of that. We moved out of state. Like my cousin Lorraine, I left home and friends and family and everything familiar in order to support my husband. Like everyone else who ever moved away—I could *now* send a Christmas newsletter! While we didn't exactly go as far as Europe or Africa, I had to convince Frank that we did indeed move far enough away (five hours by car) to justify sending one. This concept was foreign to him since most New Yorkers never leave New York, and true New Yorkers never *ever* send Christmas newsletters.

When did I send our first Christmas newsletter? It was Christmas 1996, and I remember feeling very torn about what to include in that letter. There is such a fine line between reporting good news and bragging—between catching people up and boring them to death—between giving God glory and sounding hyper-spiritual. Christians are especially diverse when it comes to the tone of their Christmas newsletters. We received one from a pastor who never mentioned God, Jesus, the virgin birth, the word Savior or anything else remotely construed as religious. He signed it "Happy Holidays," and I know for a fact that he is passionate about the Lord. Then you have Charlie Church who mentions Jesus in every sentence, quotes thirteen verses, and reminds the unsaved that they're heading straight to hell before signing off with "Have a Merry Christmas." A woman from our congregation sent one with seventeen mentions of "Jesus" and twelve "blessings." She wrote, "The children bicker and are all growing to be like Jesus. They're such a blessing. Jesus took our dog Scruffy home this past summer. Scruffy had a rare nose disease so this was a blessing. Jesus released Fred from his job last month, a mixed blessing. Remember Jesus loves you. May you be as blessed as we have been. His blessings are free—be blessed!"

What are people thinking when they write Christmas newsletters? I am always amused by the newsletters that are written entirely in the third person as if a professional journalist had done the job. "Bob's company is doing well. Alice's time is spent driving the kids around the world and cleaning up after them. Greg is going off to college in the fall. Robbie loves basketball (and girls!). Little Caitlin is a budding ballerina." Then there are those written from the perspective of the family pet with words like *purrrfect* scattered throughout. These folks include a paw print next to the signatures of family members.

Who should send Christmas newsletters and who should receive them? Miss Manners ought to set some guidelines. I, for one, do not believe that Christmas newsletters should be sent to anyone who lives within a sixty-mile radius of the sender. This year, we received three from families who attend our local church, one from a neighbor a few houses away, and two from women in the PTA. The neighbor's newsletter was a four-page, single-spaced, -professionally typeset layout with columns and nine super-sharp glossy photo images copied right onto bonded, high quality paper. There were pictures of their kids, their kids' prom dates, their vacations, their dogs, their pool, and their remodeled kitchen! They listed their favorite hobbies, books, movies, quotes, and restaurants. They listed out-of-town guests, births, and deaths. The only thing they left out was their IRS return. These people barely wave. What prompted them to send us a newsletter? (Or should I call it a newsgazette?) I had to read it in two sittings (if you know what I mean).

Why do we send Christmas newsletters? I suppose there are many reasons. We want to matter, to keep in touch, to catch up, to connect, to be remembered, to tell others we are doing fine. Many of us desire to be well liked and regarded for some aspect of life— kids, accomplishments, work—even ministry. The apostle Paul sent newsletters all the time—not just at Christmas. He exhorted us to be living letters from a loving God to a longing world. What did you write in your newsletter and if you've never written one—what *would* you write? As the saying goes, you are the only Bible some will ever read. What do people "read" when they encounter you? Jesus desires to be "sent out" every day, but He needs faithful messengers who will not grow weary in carrying His message. No matter how advanced technology becomes, humanity's search for personal significance will remain futile without the acceptance of a personal Savior. Do your friends and family know what you stand for and who you believe in? Witty words, amusing anecdotes, and pretty pictures can only go so far. The world would not be so easily distracted by tinsel, glitter, and counterfeits if the "newsletters of our lives" were credible, consistent, and Christlike. Let us resound the heartfelt cry of Isaiah.

> Then I heard the voice of the Lord saying, "Whom shall I send? And who will go for us?" And I said, "Here am I. Send me!"
>
> —Isaiah 6:8 (NIV)

32

And So This
Is Christmas

eck the halls with boughs of holly,
Fa- la- la- la- la, la- la- la- la.

Christians around the globe are facing brutal and intense persecution for their faith.

'Tis the season to be jolly, Fa- la- la- la- la-, la- la- la- la.

Few believers in America are aware of these atrocities, and even fewer seem to care.

Don we now our gay apparel, Fa- la- la-, la- la- la-, la- la- la.

For refusing to denounce Jesus Christ, people are arrested, tortured, imprisoned, beaten, raped, and killed.

Toll the ancient yuletide carol, Fa- la- la- la- la-, la- la- la- la.

Towns are pillaged, churches are burned down, homes are confiscated, and pastors disappear.

See the blazing yule before us, Fa- la- la- la- la-, la- la- la- la.

Children are ripped from parents and sold into slavery or sent to labor camps.

Strike the harp and join the chorus, Fa- la- la- la- la-, la- la- la- la.

This is happening in Communist countries: China, North Korea, Vietnam, Laos, and Cuba.

Follow me in merry measure, Fa-la-la-, la-la-la-, la, la-la.

This is happening in Islamic countries: Sudan, Pakistan, Saudi Arabia, Nigeria, Egypt, and Uzbekistan.

While I tell of yuletide treasure, Fa- la- la- la- la-, la- la- la- la.

In Iran, four prominent evangelical pastors have been abducted and assassinated in a three-year period.

Fast away the old year passes, Fa- la- la- la- la-, la- la- la- la.

In China, three evangelicals were beaten to death by police for leading house-churches.

Hail the new ye lads and lasses, Fa- la- la- la- la-, la- la- la- la.

Seven Trappist monks were taken hostage in Algeria. One of these priests was an eighty-two-year-old doctor. Two months later, their throats were slit.

Sing we joyous all together, Fa- la- la-, la- la- la-, la, la- la.

A Catholic priest in Vietnam is halfway through a twenty-year prison term for teaching adult catechism classes. Ten members of his order are serving time for the same "offense."

Heedless of the wind and weather, Fa- la- la- la- la-, la- la- la- la.

Chinese police circulated an arrest warrant that bears the names of three thousand evangelical preachers. Thousands of Christians are in Chinese prisons for "subversive" activities.

Fa- la- la- la-, la- la- la-laaaaaaaa !!!

I first learned of the massive persecution of Christians at a dinner hosted by Prison Fellowship the night before the National Prayer Breakfast. Chuck Colson shared that more Christians have been killed in the twentieth century than all nineteen previous centuries combined. *All nineteen?* That was shocking news to me. He then presented the highly esteemed William Wilberforce Award to David Horowitz, a Jew, who is senior fellow at the Hudson Institute think tank in Washington, D.C. Mr. Horowitz has worked to bring the plight of persecuted Christians to the forefront of national attention. He took the podium and proceeded to admonish, challenge, rebuke, and chastise the audience, which largely comprised the *Who's Who* of the modern Christian era, not to mention every God-fearing politician from "The Hill."

Mr. Horowitz told the rapt audience that he decided to devote time and energy to documenting and exposing Christian persecution because it reminded him of another time in fairly recent history when millions were systematically destroyed for their faith. He wondered why Christians can't, won't, or refuse to see the writing on the wall. David Horowitz wants to know why the American Christian church seems to be looking the other way. No one could give him an answer that night, but I would like to be ready with one when my children and my grandchildren ask me someday, "Why were those things allowed to happen? Why didn't the good people do something? What did you do, Grandma?"

In John Lennon's famous Christmas song, he asks,
And so this is Christmas—
And what have you done?
Another year's over—
And a new one's begun.

And what have *you* done? Beyond the burden of prayer is a call to action. Jesus left the ninety-nine to look for the one. The Good Samaritan extended love to the wounded. Paul encouraged the church to take responsibility for the well-being of fellow believers. We can find concrete ways to urge our own government to take up the cause of our persecuted brothers and sisters. May we not only pray for those who are wronged but also for strength and boldness to speak to others of the things that must be made right. Our silence will only breed evil, which ultimately destroys us all. May it never be said that we were passive, apathetic, or unmoved by the suffering of other believers. May we never grow so comfortable in freedom that we are unwilling to pray and speak out in defense of those who have paid the ultimate price for their faith.

If you are interested in learning about the persecuted church around the world, I highly recommend that you read *In the Lion's Den* by Nina Shea and *Their Blood Cries Out* by Paul Marshall.

Whenever we have the opportunity, we should do good to everyone, especially to our Christian brothers and sisters.
—Galatians 6:10 (NLT)

33

Denomination Frustration

On one warm summer evening, the family was gathered at the table out on the deck, eating one of my gourmet, two-step dinners. As usual, Frank and I asked the children about their day, hoping to improve *their* communication skills and *our* parenting skills. This verbal exchange has become one of the highlights of my day. No one is expected to provide lengthy discourse when asked what they did that particular day, but the response "nothing" is unacceptable in the Lofaro household. Frank loosened his tie and proceeded.

"Jordan, did you have a good day? What did you do?"

"Nothing." Jordan's countenance dropped a mile. My mother-heart went into gear. I placed my hand over his, which has begun to resemble a bear cub paw.

"Jordan, what's the matter, honey?"

"Nothing."

I persisted. *"What* is wrong?"

"Nothing!"

Frank grew impatient. "Jordan Lofaro, WHAT happened today?"

Paris attempted to offer some assistance. "He's mad because he got into a big argument at the pool, and these kids we know started making fun of him, and he almost punched Billy Spencer."

I was disappointed and quite surprised. Now there are a few boys at the neighborhood pool whom I can envision Jordan socking, but *not* sweet Billy Spencer whose father is the head deacon at a local church. "How could you fight with Billy? I thought you got along well with him."

Judge Frank assisted in the interrogation. "Jordan answer your mother . . . *immediately.*"

The defendant squirmed in his seat. "I *didn't* fight. I *argued.*"

Star witness Paris was happy to add details. "Oh, he argued all right. I was *so* embarrassed."

And I was so disappointed. "You ask for more privileges, so I drop you off at the pool for two hours and this is what happens?"

"Don't look at *me!*" bristled big sister Paris. *"He's* the one with the problem!"

I grew impatient. "Jordan, for the last time—WHAT problem?"

The defendant took a deep sigh and prepared to come clean. All eyes were on him.

"James wanted to know what church we go to."

Court clerk Capri perked up. "I know what church we go to! It's a snack church!"

Judge Frank smiled at her and placed his authoritative right pointer finger upon his lips. His attention turned once again toward Jordan. "What did you say to James?"

"I told him we go to Grace Covenant Church."

"And?"

"And he wanted to know what kind of church it is."

"And?"

"And I told him it was Christian. Peter O'Brien started laughing and said that was a stupid answer. I said it was just Christian, nothing else, and then they wanted to know if we were Catholic or Protestant, and I said neither, and they laughed harder and then Billy said I must be a pretty dumb Christian, so I grabbed his goggles and threw them in the pool, and he told the lifeguard, and I got a time-out, and that's all. Can I be excused now?"

Frank and I looked at each other and then we looked at Jordan and in perfectly synchronized timing, we both said, "Absolutely *not!*"

My adrenaline soared. "Jordan, we call ourselves Christians! We follow Jesus. That's *all* you need to explain. When you're born in Italy—you're Italian. When you're born in Mars—you're Martian. When you're born in Jesus Christ—you're Christian!"

"But you and Dad weren't born Christian. At least you had a religion!"

Star witness Paris became star sympathizer. "He's right. People *always* ask me what kind of Christians we are."

I was mildly flabbergasted. "What *kind* of Christians? I'll tell you what *kind* of Christians! Try capital *C!* Authentic! Original! First century! Do you think the early Christians needed additional titles? They didn't throw Baptists and Methodists and Nazarenes to the lions! They threw *Christians* to the lions! Do you think it was Catholics and Protestants who followed Jesus from town to town and saw him bodily raised from the dead? Do you think being Pentecostal or Presbyterian will automatically get you into heaven? No way! We're Christians! We follow Jesus! Christians! Period! Got it?"

Judge Frank saw that I had gotten "a bit" emotional and asked for quiet in the court. "Jordan, there is nothing wrong with titles and denominations, but more often than not, these have separated people and caused division and strife. We don't believe Jesus ever intended for Christians to be splintered the way we are. Scripture says the world will know us by the love we have for one another, but I think God is pretty disappointed with us."

Jordan was not yet satisfied.

"But Dad, everybody is *some* type of Christian."

"Listen, buddy. The term 'Christian' is used in many ways. Some use the label 'Christian' to refer to people who are not Jewish, Muslim, or Buddhist. Some say Christians killed people in the Crusades, the Inquisition, and the Holocaust. The truth is that a genuine Christian loves Jesus and obeys His commandments. Your Mom and I are doing our best to be true Christians. We have no need for any additional classification concerning our faith. You will eventually make your own choice about that."

That Frank—always so calm and rational. It really bugs me.

"I know, Dad. I already made my own choice. You and Mom know I love Jesus."

"Son, would you prefer to say you are a Judeo-Christian or an Orthodox Christian or something along those lines?"

Jordan looked at Frank and then at his sisters and landed his freshly thawed gaze upon me. "Nope. From now on I'm going to tell people we're 'Over-Excited Christians.'"

Judge Frank, star witness Paris, court clerk Capri, and defendant Jordan all burst into laughter, and I believe it was coming in my direction. Fine with me. Court was adjourned and we went out for ice cream.

"In essentials, unity. In nonessentials, liberty. In all things, charity."

—Philip Melanchton

So you are all children of God through faith in Christ Jesus. And all who have been united with Christ in baptism have been made like him. There is no longer Jew or Gentile, slave or free, male or female. For you are all Christians—you are one in Christ Jesus.

—Galatians 3:26-28 (NLT)

34

A Love Letter to My Children

December 25, 1999

Dear Children,

Just wanted to write and let you know that Dad and I are about halfway through our "parenting years." Don't get alarmed—we'll *always* be your parents. This doesn't mean we're quitting in 2009. It just means that our toting, tickling, training, teaching time with you is half done. People told us it would fly by much too quickly, but we didn't believe them. When you were babies, it felt as though some nights lasted forever. When you became toddlers, we hoped time would slow down a bit, but it didn't. Your baby teeth are all gone, none of you talk like Tweety Bird, and you never play dress-up anymore. Thank God for memories.

We dedicated each of you at the altar of the church, surrounded by many witnesses. When you turned two, you were enrolled in Sunday school, and you've been there ever since. We sent you to Christian day camps, sports camps, and overnight camps. We carpooled you to lock-ins, youth groups, choir rehearsals, drama nights, community cleanups, outreaches, overnights, and pizza parties. We have explained what the pastors do and how you can pray for them, and we've talked about practical ways you could be helpful to others. We watched with a million emotions when the three of you decided to be baptized at the same time. Thank God for the church.

When we sponsored a child through World Vision, we watched as you took such a genuine interest in Tapiwa and as you rejoiced in the fact that she would receive the things she needed to live a productive life in Zimbabwe. When we sent Bibles to Christians in the underground church in China, you were upset to hear some of the stories we shared with you about the suffering of Christians around the world, whose only crime was believing in Jesus. You guys wanted to fly to Sudan immediately to "buy freedom" for one hundred Christians slaves. You have become acquainted with the Angel Tree program of Prison Fellowship and have clearly understood how sad Christmas can be for a kid whose mom or dad is in prison. Your hearts have been enlarged. Thank God for effective ministries.

You have met many wonderful people who love the Lord and serve Him well. Some have sat at our dinner table, some have stood in the pulpit, and some have spoken from microphones three hundred yards away. You have gleaned much from their preaching, their teaching, their music, their mission, their passion. Some of the people who have benefited you are well known, and some are only known by those whom they quietly, faithfully serve. Thank God for real heroes.

The bittersweet reality is that the years of Big Bird, Barney, and bubble baths are over. You don't believe in the Tooth Fairy, the Great Pumpkin, or the fat guy in red, (although we have gone to great lengths to teach you the true story of the remarkable Christian man named Nicholas of Lycea).

Your formal education is also at a halfway mark. You've observed how easily kids are swayed by friends, music, and clothing ads. Words such as genocide, homicide, and suicide are no longer foreign. You've begun to believe school shootings are a regular occurrence in America. You have learned what "the system" has to say about AIDS, safe sex, alcohol, and drugs. You have heard what other kids think about dating, lying, MTV, and Pokemon. Sadly, some of the famous people you look up to have failed in their "personal" lives. Nobody seems to refer to any of this as "sin." Thank God for absolute truth.

We have checked off a lot of boxes on that ever-growing list entitled, "How to Raise Christian Kids." We bought you "all the right stuff": Christian books, videos, CDs, games, jewelry, and shirts. We keep replacing your Bibles with age-appropriate ones, and Dad does a terrific job holding your attention during family devotions. However, we will *never* be able to convey all the things we think you'll need to know in order to be prepared for life. We had no way of knowing what current events would be hurled in front of your young eyes and ears, and we can't predict what issues will come about as a result of natural disasters, advanced technology, and a culture that's becoming morally numb. Sometimes, we feel discouraged because we haven't even begun to scratch the surface of what we want you to know. Thank God for grace.

In addition to doing a lot of things right—we've also managed to "blow it" on countless occasions. We are embarrassed about the times you have seen Daddy and me display selfish attitudes and speak harsh words. At times we have used poor judgment and often shown you our own inadequacies. We never wanted to pass down our smelly garbage, but we have managed to do just that. When we don't like some of the things you say or do—guess who it reminds us of? We will continue to ask for guidance and forgiveness. Thank God for mercy.

The dawn of the new millennium happens to mark the halftime of your childhood. Dad and I want to be absolutely sure you fully understand these few things. . . Jesus sees you and knows you and loves you with an everlasting love that cannot be defined or measured. You were created to know Him and to make Him known. Whether you live on a mountain in Timbuktu, or in the White House, or in suburbia, your life will be mediocre, at best, if you are not intimate with God.

You will *never* have true success if you do not have true faith. You will *never* become a fine leader until you become a fine servant. You will never know deep joy without knowing the meaning of the very first Christmas. A Savior was born. A King

was given. He is the best gift you will *ever* receive. His name is
Jesus.

Merry Christmas, dear children.

I love you.

Who shall separate us from the love of Christ?
Shall trouble or hardship or persecution or
famine or nakedness or danger or sword? No, in all
these things we are more than conquerors through
him who loved us. For I am convinced that neither
death nor life, neither angels nor demons, neither the
present nor the future, nor any powers, neither height
nor depth, nor anything else in all creation, will be
able to separate us from the love of God that is in
Christ Jesus our Lord.

—Romans 8:35, 37-39 (NIV)

35

Millennium Memories

Millennium Eve. Some feared it. A few celebrated it in a very lavish way. Others tried to downplay it. Many were quite comfortable with their plans to stay home and do absolutely nothing about it. Then there were those who completely ignored it and went to bed before midnight. After all, wasn't it just another New Year's Eve?

Maybe—but not for me. You see, the turn of a millennium only happens once every ... well ... you know, and I wanted to make a memory. I wanted to taste, touch, see, smell, and hear the arrival of the next thousand years with color, panache, and flair. I wanted to be somewhere that would be marked in the history books. I wanted to look back and sigh with nostalgia when I pondered 01-01-00. I wanted my children to have it etched in the recesses of their minds. I only had one problem. My husband wanted to spend the stroke of midnight in the basement watching TV, eating chips, and banging pots and pans. The TV and chips didn't disturb me too much, but I felt serious conflict about our children's memory of the new millennium involving pots and pans.

It was December 30, 1999. We made our annual Christmas rounds on Long Island and spent two wonderful days in Manhattan taking in the tree, the windows, and a show.

We departed the hotel at noon to drive home to Virginia, and we passed through Times Square, which was being readied for the following night. The dazzling Waterford crystal ball was lifted and lowered in a dress rehearsal of sorts.

I wasn't asking to be at the Pyramids, the Parthenon, or Paris on Millennium Eve. It's not even that I wanted to be in Times Square. I had never, in my thirty-seven years as a resident of New York, had the slightest desire to spend New Year's Eve in Times Square, but I was drawn in by all the excitement. I knew it was out of the question. But it was fun to imagine what two million people, eight thousand police officers, and several tons of confetti would look like exactly thirty-six hours from that moment in time. I just didn't want to be in the basement.

When we pulled into our driveway soon after dark, we were still unsure of how we would spend the next night. Washington, D.C., was putting on its very own extravaganza at the Lincoln Memorial, but earlier in the month, a friend of a neighbor of a cousin of a guy from the park police told us they had been getting terrorist threats. When I awoke the next morning, I felt a calm indifference about Millennium Eve. Many churches decided not to hold services, most local restaurants were booked to capacity, and some people had begun their final Y2K preparations. I could hear bathtubs being filled for miles around. It was a sleepy day. I read, meditated upon honoring one's husband, played Mousetrap, cleaned the oven, and took a nap. As I dozed off, I reflected on my many blessings—health, peace, joy, and the love of family, friends, and God.

I literally experienced a rude awakening as I opened my eyes to see Frank standing on top of the den table banging a pot lid against a frying pan. He smirked boyishly and seemed quite pleased with himself. He cleared his throat and banged and clanged. My peace slipped away as I sat up, half dazed.

"Frank, why didn't you wake me? You let me miss the new year? How *could* you? I can't believe you let me sleep that long!"

Frank stared back with a look of puzzlement. "Whaddya talkin' about, Ellie—it's only 6:00. You napped for two hours. Wake up!"

"Why are you banging that pot?"

"I am banging it to make an announcement."

"What announcement?"

"I've decided we're going to the Lincoln Memorial for the festivities!!!"

"You're kidding. What about the terrorists?"

"They're all in New York."

"Frank, what happened? I thought you were determined to stay home tonight."

"I was, but I've had a change of heart. You're right, honey. We need to make a memory. Everybody up! Who's hungry?"

He didn't have to convince *me!* We all got excited about our newly established destination. The kids ate macaroni and cheese while Frank and I ate sushi rolls and leftover pastrami from Carnegie Deli (always our last stop in NYC). We dressed in layers and drove into the nation's capital. By the looks of Route 66 at nine o'clock that night, the Rapture had taken place. We sailed to D.C. in a record twenty-two minutes.

The mile-long strip of grass known as "The Mall" between the Lincoln and Washington Memorials was filling quickly, and we found our spot just as the televised portion of "America's Millennium" was about to begin. Excitement certainly filled the chilly night air. A host of renowned artists shared their gifts. At midnight, a spectacular fireworks display ran down the Lincoln Memorial steps, across the Reflecting Pool, up the Washington Memorial, and out into the night sky. As the fireworks subsided, we sang "America the Beautiful," and from where we were huddled that night, it truly was.

Sleep came. January 1, 2000 came. So did the rest of the month. Bank statements, bills, paychecks, electricity, water, and food all came. Girl Scouts came to sell cookies. Firemen came to collect donations. Friends came to visit. I guess you could say it was just another January. The predictions of doom surrounding Y2K never came to pass. I'm thankful for that, but as believers, we know that none of us can know exactly what the future will bring. By God's grace, though we will have tragedy, sickness, and sorrow, yet we will also have celebration, joy, and confidence. Whatever the state of affairs in the world or in our hearts, God will still be God. He holds the future. So I enter the third millennium with peace because He is a good and loving God. One day, the eternal New Year will be launched in the eternal New Jerusalem, and what a celebration that will be! God will be on His throne, and those who love Him will gather around. Until then—I'll occupy, I'll serve, I'll preach and teach, and I'll set my face toward the Son.

Let us not become weary in doing good, for at the proper time we will reap a harvest if we do not give up.

—Galatians 6:9 (NIV)

36

The Holy Dread

There are so many "isms" in this modern world. Some are glorious. Others are evil. Many are misunderstood. There is one particular "ism" that seems to strike a raw nerve among many Christians. I'm speaking of "evangelism." That single word may cause some Christians to break out into a cold sweat and others to take off running. The rest either do the dirty "chore" reluctantly, nervously recite a three-point plan, or honestly believe that, thank God, that's not their particular gift.

The fact remains that there are Christians who wax cold at the mention of it. Call me crazy, but words like guilt, fear, and dread come to mind. Some feel guilt because they have never participated in evangelism (except for the tract they left at the diner that one night). Others experience fear because of the risk of rejection, anxiety about what to say, and the courage to get started. And still others dread the worst. "I don't want to look like a nut from some cult," or "I don't want to push my beliefs on other people." Then there are those who recite Ephesians 4:11 and are convinced that evangelism is a special calling for a chosen few.

To make things worse, evangelism is suffering from a lot of bad press. Some people have been terribly traumatized by throat stuffers, while others have been badly bruised by Bible bangers. On the other end of the spectrum, some believers leave thirsty people parched because they view faith as being too personal. Too personal? I grew up with that nonsense. Nobody mentioned God because nobody had anything to say about God. How can you fall in love and not tell anybody? How can you have knowledge of a cure and not share it with those who are in pain? How dare we minimize what Jesus accomplished on the cross? The Son of God hung nailed, naked, and battered. Too personal?

Unfortunately, we have all witnessed the angry Christian sharing anything *but* love with the potential convert. The average American TV viewer who surfs hundreds of channels observes a wide range of evangelical "styles." In spite of the blows suffered in the past, I have great respect for most televangelists.

However, a few need to get off the air and back into the prayer closet. I personally struggle with the guys who add a syllable to the Lord's name . . . *"Jeees-us-uh"* and with those whose hairpieces need revival.

So, if both Christians and nonChristians often feel uncomfortable with evangelism, how then are we to respond to the Great Commission? Although how-to booklets, four-point tracts, two-question tests, and high-tech videos have their place, nothing can substitute for the efficacy of the human factor. I'm speaking of caring, one-to-one relationships. It's called "lifestyle evangelism." It takes time and costs more in terms of personal investment. Are you willing to develop relationships with nonChristians, or have you retreated to a comfortable Christian subculture? Separatism is one of those frightening "isms."

It often requires us to slow down in our life routines and to show more of an interest in the people we meet. It took me nine visits to her line, but I have finally been able to share God's love with the single mom at the supermarket checkout. The house painters came every day for four days. I got a fresh coat, and they got a fresh revelation. When we placed our children into a wonderful public elementary school last year, I invited the entire office staff to a Christmas tea with a sumptuous dessert buffet. I said grace and shared words of life and sent each kind woman off with a dessert in one hand and a devotional book in the other. The florist, the FedEx guy, the hair stylist, the person in the nearby cubicle, the wild cousin, the next-door neighbor—people need the Lord.

The greatest of all Christian evangelists wrote, "For I am not ashamed of the gospel of Christ, for it is the power of God to salvation," (Romans 1:16, NKJV). As its source, evangelism must flow from a heart of love. Of all the gifts, love is the greatest. Love should not be something that we fake because of guilt. Instead, when we love, we simply allow the Holy Spirit to love through us. Are you ready to love those who need to hear the Good News? When you can answer with a resounding "Yes!" then evangelism will be a joy. Communicating your faith will be something you cannot help but do.

If you are interested in reading more on evangelism, I highly recommend the following books:

Out of the Saltshaker and into the World by Rebecca Manley Pippert

Gentle Persuasion by Joseph Aldrich

Conspiracy of Kindness by Steve Sjogren

How to Give Away Your Faith by Paul Little

Powerful Evangelism for the Powerless by C. John Miller.

How, then, can they call on the one they have not believed in? And how can they believe in the one of whom they have not heard? And how can they hear without someone preaching to them? And how can they preach unless they are sent? As it is written, "How beautiful are the feet of those who bring good news!"

—Romans 10:14-15 (NIV)

37

Estrogen Issues

Remember the first time you heard that eggs are bad for your health? It was a sad day for chicken farmers and egg lovers everywhere. Then they added butter to the list and then red meat and then—well, that list changes every month, and quite frankly, I'm having a hard time keeping up with all those university reports. We switched to margarine, and now margarine is said to be more harmful than butter. We started eating more fish, and now there are dangerous levels of toxins in some seafood thanks to industrial progress. We've cut down on soda and started drinking more apple juice, only to learn that there are chemicals on, in, and around the apples. What's a woman to do?

Like it or not, we are living in the Information Age. (Too much information, if you ask me!) Cholesterol, fat grams, trans fat, saturated fat, LDL, HDL—I liked the days when the only thing that was bad for you was too much dessert—and even that was permissible on special occasions.

I become dizzy in supermarket aisles: olive oil, sunflower oil, vegetable oil, palm-kernel oil, coconut oil, peanut oil, hydrogenated oil. Less fat, low fat, no fat. Lite, lean, little. Snackwell, Smart Start, Healthy Choice. You need a degree in nutrition to wade through the jungle of label lingo. And what about the vitamin aisle? I long to return to the days when there were only two choices: One-A-Day or Flintstones. My friend Sue is taking ginseng for memory. Debbie is drinking blue-green algae. And Karen is ingesting Bee Alive for more energy. Do I need beta-carotene? Will iron make me constipated? What about chromium or B12?

I had just completed my annual exam the week of my forty-second birthday, and my gynecologist asked me if I was getting enough calcium. She looked very concerned.

"Ellie, you're entering a season of life when you need to be more concerned about certain issues such as your calcium intake."

"Don't worry about me. I'm a big milk drinker."

"How much milk do you drink?"

"At least a glass a day," I proudly retorted.

"You should be getting at least 1000 milligrams of calcium each day; a cup of milk has 300 mg. How *else* do you get calcium?"

I squirmed a bit on the table. "Uhhh . . . I eat broccoli?"

"Sorry. Only 36 milligrams in a half cup. I do not want to alarm you, but without enough calcium, you will be at high risk for osteoporosis."

"Okay, you have my attention. What do you recommend?"

"Take two Extra-Strength Tums daily."

"Tums? Even without a stomachache?" I had a strange sense that a Tums commercial was being filmed via hidden camera. The good doctor stood to her feet.

"When you return for your exam next year, we'll begin to discuss a premenopausal regimen."

"But I'm only forty-two!"

"It's never too early to become educated. I'll explain some of your options."

Options . . . hmmm. The cooking oil suddenly became the least of my concerns.

Options. I believe that was a nice word for Hormone Replacement Therapy (HRT). Estrogen, progestin, androgen, and clonidine. Menopause never conjures attractive images. I've heard many sagas about mood swings, bladder infections, loss of muscle tone, dry skin, osteoporosis (not if I take my Tums), and those dreaded hot flashes. I'm told that they are no laughing matter.

Somewhat disconcerting are the warnings on the products that are prescribed to women dealing with menopause. The ads are definitely double-edged.

"Evista can help you (but there are side effects such as hot flashes and leg cramps)."

"The Climara patch is so easy to use. Just put it on once a week and forget it. (There are possible side effects such as headaches, nausea, fluid retention, irregular bleeding, and breast tenderness.)"

"FemPatch . . . for when a little estrogen is right for her. (Warning: Estrogen has been reported to increase the risk of endometrial carcinoma in some women.)"

What did women do before all of these modern break-throughs? No wonder my grandmother never came out of the kitchen. Our beloved sisters in Scripture were probably not getting proper HRT! Maybe Miriam murmured against Moses because she needed a boost of estrogen. Who knows what hormonal deficiency afflicted Lot's wife. And poor Martha—she may have been having a hot flash each time she ran out of the room. I attempted to convey these new concerns to Frank, but he seemed unsympathetic and somewhat patronizing. Just wait until he needs Viagra.

Note: Although I have periodic apprehension about health concerns and the aging process, I closely follow the AMA's recommendations for women over forty, and I encourage all sisters to do the same. Prevention sure beats treatment. Get thee to thine annual exam!

Even to your old age and gray hairs I am he, I am he who will sustain you. I have made you and I will carry you; I will sustain you and I will rescue you.
—Isaiah 46:4 (NIV)

38

Good-bye (For Now)

I t ended as most women's retreats do. Hugs. Clasped arms and hands. Tears of joy, of hope, of surrender. Renewed faith. Proclamations. Newly made promises to self, family, and God. Resolutions. Determination to keep them. A deeper sense of the Lord's love and mercy. The altar was deep and wide with women bowing, kneeling, sitting, praying, singing, and weeping.

I always come away from women's gatherings in awe of God. Being the guest speaker is both exhilarating and exhausting. It is a privilege that I pray I'll never take for granted. I am always humbled by the idea that women are coming to "fill up" for a weekend and that I've been asked to hold the nozzle. There is a holy fear about filling their tanks sloppily, pouring too much or too little. I am sober about the judgment I bring on myself should I serve something watered-down or contaminated.

Most women had exited the sanctuary to go to the wonderful luncheon that awaited. A few lingered to finish their conversations with God and one another. A sweet, diminutive woman whom I had never met approached me slowly. She had a certain pain in her eyes, which were moist as she spoke. Her head tilted a bit to one side as she shyly inched closer.

"Someone told me you know Kathy Troccoli."

"Yes, as a matter of fact, I do."

"Do you know her well?"

"Yes, *very* well."

The woman looked encouraged. "Would you give her a message for me?"

"Of course, I'd be happy to."

Her warm blue eyes filled and a tear ran down the center of each cheek. "I lost my daughter six months ago, and Kathy's song 'Goodbye for Now' has given me strength and courage. There were some nights when I didn't think I would ever handle the grief or make it till the morning. That song has blessed my family and me more than anyone will ever know. Will you tell her for me?"

"I promise I will. It really *is* an anointed song, isn't it? I've one. I know that was Kathy's hope when she wrote it. She is certainly familiar with grief. She has buried her parents, her grandparents, and recently her aunt. Cancer is prevalent in their family history, but Kathy has chosen faith over fear. She is one of those people who looks forward to a big reunion!"

I smiled, hoping I hadn't sounded like Pollyanna. I didn't know where to take the conversation from there. Six months is so recent—so raw. What condition would I be in after the death of a child? Would I attend a women's retreat? Would I put myself around so many women who had endless stories (and photos) of their children? I was hesitant to ask about her daughter. Yet, I have often been told that grieving people need to talk about the person whom they miss so badly.

"What was your daughter's name? Did she have your pretty eyes?"

The woman wiped her nose with a crushed, damp tissue and offered a half smile. "Cindy was only twenty-one. It's been *so* hard." My thoughts raced, and I wondered if her daughter had died in a car accident or if she had lost a battle with cancer. I returned the half smile and squeezed the weary mother's arm.

"I am so sorry. How wonderful that you've come here this weekend to be encouraged. How is the rest of the family doing?"

"Her younger brother is taking it the worst. You see, Cindy was bipolar, and we all suffered with it the last ten years. She had good times and bad ones. She loved the Lord, but she got tired of her struggle. Every day had become a painful battle. She lost the will to go on. We know she is with the Lord. That is why Kathy's song has been so meaningful to all of us." The sweet face suddenly seemed pained, as if something had jabbed her. "Cindy took her own life."

The woman's shoulders started to shudder and I stepped closer so my hands were now cupping each of her forearms. Her eyes searched mine for permission to go on with her heartbreaking account. I nodded reassuringly. "Who found her?" I asked.

"It was a nightmare I thought would never end. Her body was recovered four days after she jumped to her death from the Brooklyn Bridge. We found a letter and a journal. She was just tired. She gave up. I would give anything to hug her one more time. How I wish we could have her back. We can't . . . for now. But . . . someday."

"Yes," I whispered, "someday." I held the stranger-turned-sister for a long minute, and our warm tears ran together. She cried for her daughter and I cried for *her.* And I think I cried for *me.* I thought of my four grandparents and especially of my sweet "Nona," whom I sorely miss. I thought of Judy Raftery and Lorraine Hansen and Martha Loredo and Eleanor Nash and Linda Roiland and Phyllis Caroleo and Kathy Fardig. No camera crews arrived when these special women passed away. No monuments were built, no lengthy obituaries were written. They weren't celebrities by the world's standards, but they were shining stars to their families and friends . . . and to me.

> I can't believe that you're really gone now
> Seems like it's all just a dream.
> How can it be that the world will go on
> When something has died within me?
> But there will be a time when I'll see your face
> And I'll hear your voice and there we will laugh again.
> And there will come a day when I'll hold you close
> No more tears to cry cause we'll have forever.
> But I'll say goodbye for now.[2]

$\mathscr{A}$nd I heard a loud voice from the throne saying, "Now the dwelling of God is with men, and he will live with them. They will be his people, and God himself will be with them and be their God. He will wipe every tear from their eyes. There will be no more death or mourning or crying or pain, for the old order of things has passed away."

—Revelation 21:3-4 (NIV)

39

God Bless America

$\mathcal{L}$ eaving New York was a huge adjustment for me. The kids didn't miss a beat: same swing set, different yard. Frank didn't suffer either. Men are often defined by what they do, and Chuck Colson gave him plenty to do. That left me. I experienced the "woe is me" syndrome. My closest friends were far away. My Italian family could no longer pop over (with real food). I had to find a new gynecologist. Our new church was very small, and when I asked about VBS, they suggested that I launch one. This shocked me, in light of the fact that our church that we attended for fifteen years in New York had two thousand members, thirty-four ministries, and a camera-ready worship service.

Living outside the nation's fast-paced financial hub certainly influenced our lives in some interesting ways. Living outside the nation's fast paced political hub has *also* influenced us in some interesting ways. Buying a house thirty minutes from the capital allows us to take a lot of day drips. Discovering D.C. has become a very enjoyable pastime for the Lofaro family.

If you're like me and too lazy to read fat books about the history of a city, then do the next best thing: take a Gray Line Tour! They're very educational, and the whole family will enjoy the air-conditioned bus complete with lavatory. (Moms, they don't serve snacks, so bring your own.) Hosting out-of-town friends and family has resulted in my becoming a reasonably informed citizen. After many walking tours through museums and monuments as well as five bus excursions, I have finally begun to get a handle on this place.

For me, Washington, D.C., used to be a destination for overnight school trips or Campus Life kids. I never imagined I would ever live nearby. Nor did I realize that relearning history would cause me to become such an enthusiastic patriot. Though you'll never see my name on a DAR roster, I have certainly developed a heightened sense of pride in our country's heritage.

D.C. is a beautiful city. The influences of French and English architects are seen everywhere. Crossing the Memorial Bridge conjures images of crossing the Seine by Paris's Rive Gauche. No building stands taller than the Capitol dome, which is quite a sharp contrast to the Manhattan skyline. There are parks and monuments galore. The greenery surrounding the federal buildings is impeccably manicured. There is no admission charge for the museums of the Smithsonian Institute or the National Zoo or the many fascinating tours in the federal buildings and monuments.

The District of Columbia has twenty-six police forces present at all times. The District has one. The President has one. The embassies have one. The CIA has one. The Pentagon has one. The FBI has one . . . you get the picture. Needless to say, we feel fairly safe walking the Mall. (No, not *that* mall!)

D.C. is crawling with politicians, past, present, and wannabes. They say it's hard to tell who your real friends are in a city like this one. The Republicans and Democrats socialize with each other and even attend prayer meetings together. At the President's Prayer Breakfast, I learned that some of these weekly meetings began taking place before I was born. Some of the most well respected Christians on "The Hill" happen to be leaders within the Democratic Party. Don't tell the people who think God is a Republican.

I believe we have been truly blessed as a nation because of our Judeo-Christian foundation. The principles set forth by our founding fathers are clearly based on the inerrant and timeless strength of God's Word. Unfortunately, His mandates have been acknowledged less and less these past few decades. Americans have paid a price. Many historians have compared us to the late, not-so-great Roman Empire. Can it be?

A D.C. historian told me the nation's capital city was planned and developed so the most prominent structures would outline the shape of Christ's cross. The Capitol building is the head. The Washington Monument is the heart. The White House is the right hand; the Jefferson Memorial is the left. Years later, the perfectly symmetrical formation was finalized with the placement of the Lincoln Memorial at the foot of the cross.

Congress began each day with prayer back then, and they still do. Magnificent art depicting biblical accounts can be seen everywhere. Robert E. Lee was a devout Christian and did not personally support slavery. He was the head of his class at West Point and Lincoln's first choice to lead the north into battle. Lee declined because of familial allegiance. (They did *not* teach us that in NY!) Jamestown, Georgetown, Annapolis, and Fredericksburg were all named for British royals and established under the auspices of the Ten Commandments. Their civil law drew directly from God's law.

Until WWI, Bibles were a staple of military issue, and the inscription of the soldier's name inside the cover identified the dead. George Washington, Thomas Jefferson, Benjamin Franklin, Abraham Lincoln, and the like spoke of God every time they delivered public oration. *Lincoln's Devotionals* is in print and should become a part of your family library. Vibrant ministries bring the gospel and provide discipleship to people on Capitol Hill every day. God is working in the lives of those whom we casually or cruelly dismiss to hell.

This year as we celebrate over 225 years as "one nation under God." Our fabric may have some wrinkles, but Old Glory is still very much intact. May those who seek God join hearts and hands so that we can navigate through even the darkest night.

Let us affirm together the words of Irving Berlin (1888–1989) in his famous anthem, "God Bless America."

God Bless America,
Land that I love.
Stand beside her and guide her
Through the night with a light from above.

*I*f My people who are called by My name will
humble themselves, and pray and seek My face, and
turn from their wicked ways, then I will hear from
heaven, and will forgive their sin and heal their land.
—2 Chronicles 7:14 (NKJV)

40

Rephidim

The guest speaker told our congregation that Moses spent the first forty years of his life thinking he was somebody ... the next forty realizing he was nobody ... and the forty after that discovering what God could accomplish through a humble nobody. This analysis was of great interest to me, especially in light of the fact that I have embarked upon "the second forty."

Life as I knew it came to a startling halt when my husband accepted a position with a ministry based in the Washington, D.C., area. I had spent my entire life within a twenty-five mile radius, enjoying deep roots, a long history, and a wide comfort zone. As I shared in the opening essay, my sojourn south was the beginning of a humbling process, a pruning season in my life.

Nothing was familiar. There were no points of reference, warm fuzzies, or meaningful memories. I found it difficult to gain entry or to feel connected. I had "performed" well in the past, and I resolved to do so again. I decided the solution was to make meaningful contributions to the school, the church, and the community. Surely my gifts would be appreciated and welcomed. Surely the school board, the PTA, and the women's ministry would see that I had leadership skills and a wealth of experience. They would be glad for what I could contribute.

On the contrary, it took a few years before I felt "at home." I longed for the unconditional love that I had received so much of at one time. In my new surroundings, my motives were questioned, and my strengths were regarded by some as weaknesses. I felt like I was in a dry, forsaken desert . . . and oh, so thirsty. *God, why would you bring me out here to die?*

His response came in bits and pieces, sometimes with a gentle brush stroke and other times with a fierce sword. I was forced to come to terms with some difficult truths—mainly about myself. I had been "religious" about avoiding the "deadly sins," yet I was guilty of the *most* deadly sin: pride. When asked about my faith, I always responded, "I am not religious—but I do have a relationship." Yet, that is exactly what I had become: religious. I knew I would never be a genuine leader until I learned to be a genuine servant. Thankfully, I was sought, caught, and sidelined by a Shepherd who lovingly gave me a temporary limp.

In Exodus 17, Moses comes to the place known as *Rephidim.* A wise and godly woman once told me that *Rephidim* represents the end of ourselves—the place where we learn the limits of our own abilities—where God alone can fulfill our needs. I have spent forty years avoiding *Rephidim,* but now that I'm here, I think I'll stay. It's a hard road, but a sure one. There will be no more wandering for me.

said to the Lord, "You are my Lord; apart from you I have no good thing."

—Psalm 16:2 (NIV)

Notes

[1] From "For the Love of You." Lyrics by Margaret Becker. *Never for Nothing.* (His Eye Music: 1986).

[2] From "Goodbye for Now." Lyrics by Kathy Troccoli. *Corner of Eden.* (Sony/ATV Tunes LLC: 1998).

Speaking Engagements

To inquire about having Ellie speak at your event, call or write to:
Ellie Lofaro
PO Box 9292
Reston, VA 20195
Phone/Fax 703.435.5334
Website: www.ellielofaro.com
E-Mail: ellie@ellielofaro.com

The Proverbs 31 Woman
Running the Race of Life
The Gift of Encouragement
Joy in the Journey (Philippians)
Amazing Grace
What Is That In Your Hand?
Dealing with Change
How's Your Love Life? (Corinthians)
The Romance of Ruth
More of You Lord, Less of Me
The "Me" God Sees
Circle of Friends
The Faithfulness of God (Joshua)
A Woman of Prayer

How to Give Away Your Faith
Being a Peacemaker
The Seasons of Life
Discovering Your God-given Gifts
Communication in Marriage
Magnificent Motherhood
Becoming a Whole Woman
Leaving a Legacy
Stress or Rest?
Forgiveness Is for Giving
Sweet Fruits of the Spirit
The Princess Bride
Leaving a Legacy

Specific Requests Are Welcome